IN THE SHADOW OF THE CLOUD

PHOTOGRAPHS & HISTORIES OF
AMERICA'S ATOMIC VETERANS

WITHDRAWN
JIM LERAGER

ESSAYS BY
DR. KARL Z. MORGAN
DR. SUSAN D. LAMBERT

FULCRUM, INC.
GOLDEN, COLORADO

cover and book design by
Chris Bierwirth

front cover background photograph
used with permission by United Press International

front cover inset photography by
Jim Lerager

back cover photography
courtesy of Larry Pray

back flap photography
courtesy of Andy Partos

Copyright © 1988
by Jim Lerager

LIBRARY OF CONGRESS CATALOGING-IN-PUBLICATION DATA
Lerager, Jim, 1945–
In the Shadow of the Cloud

Bibliography: p.
1. Veterans—Diseases—United States.
2. Veterans—United States—Biography.
3. Nuclear weapons testing victims—United States—Biography.
I. Title.
UB369.L47   1988   355.1'156'0973   [B]   87-33682
ISBN 1-55591-030-0

All Rights Reserved
1 2 3 4 5 6 7 8 9 0

Printed in Singapore

Dedicated to Al and Jackie Maxwell.

This book, like all books, is in truth a collaboration. Many people have contributed to its completion and success in many ways. I wish to thank all of you, with special thanks to Dorothy Legaretta, the National Association of Radiation Survivors, and all the veterans and families who allowed me so deeply into their lives. A portion of the proceeds of this book will go to establish a fund for the widows and children of atomic veterans.

Table of Contents

1	Introduction
11	The Long Death
	Marge Piercy
12	Dale and Doris Beaman, son Doug
14	Rudy Florentine, Joanna, Susan and Rudy Jr.
16	Kay Hinkle, daughters Patti and Holly
18	Robert and Dorothea Desbien with children Robin, Robert Jr. and Emil
20	Joan McCarthy
22	Herman and Elva Tinsley
24	Frank, Marcia, Tim and Margaret Pazel
26	George and Rita Seabron
28	Walter Hooke
30	Don and Margaret Cordray
32	Bill and Jane Dolan, daughter Nancy
34	Chelo Amaro
36	Donald Rutan, daughter Wendy
38	Anthony and Mary Guarisco
40	Geri Spang and Jeff McAllister
42	Al and Jackie Maxwell
44	Tim Nuzum
46	Ben and Patricia Fudge
48	Barry and Betty Kail
50	Larry Pray, mother Helen
52	Harvey and Margaret Kokka, son Ken
54	Burney Durkin
56	Leon Walker
58	John Delay
60	Robert Campbell
62	Donna Smith-Harrison and husband, Sam

64	Jim, Barrie, Kelly and Kevin Benson
66	Robert and Barbara Jackson
68	Jim and Annamarie Nash
70	Alfredo Bautista
72	Tom and Dorothea Rose
74	Tom and Judy Smith
76	Fleaming and Lily Folsom
78	Manuel Salangsang, speaking about his father, Adriano
80	Marthann Conner and son, Charlie
82	Colonel Langdon Harrison
84	Casey and Susan Wnorowski
86	Pat Brody
88	Reason and Lois Warehime
92	Jim and Jean Dennis
98	Announced U.S. Atmospheric Nuclear Tests
99	Who is the Enemy?
	Dr. Karl Z. Morgan
105	Patriots All
	Dr. Susan D. Lambert
110	Afterword
113	Publisher's Note

List of Photographs

1	Shot Baker, Bikini Atoll, July 25, 1946, courtesy of the U.S. Navy
2	Test Shot, courtesy of Larry Pray
4	Underwater Nuclear Test, the Pacific Ocean, courtesy of Marthann Conner
5	Anthony Guarisco
6	George Seabron
7	Kay Hinkle
8	Doug Beaman
9	Rudy Florentine Jr.
13	Dale, Doris and Doug Beaman
15	Rudy Florentine, Joanna, Susan and Rudy Jr.
17	Kay Hinkle, daughters Patti and Holly
19	Robert and Dorothea Desbien with children Robin, Robert Jr. and Emil
21	Joan McCarthy
23	Herman and Elva Tinsley
25	Frank, Marcia, Tim and Margaret Pazel
27	George and Rita Seabron
29	Walter Hooke
31	Don and Margaret Cordray
33	Bill and Jane Dolan, daughter Nancy
35	Chelo Amaro
37	Donald Rutan, daughter Wendy
39	Anthony and Mary Guarisco
41	Geri Spang and Jeff McAllister
43	Al and Jackie Maxwell
45	Tim Nuzum
47	Ben and Patricia Fudge
49	Barry and Betty Kail
51	Larry Pray, mother Helen
53	Harvey and Margaret Kokka, son Ken

55	Burney Durkin
57	Leon Walker
59	John Delay
61	Robert Campbell
63	Donna Smith-Harrison and husband, Sam
65	Jim, Barrie, Kelly and Kevin Benson
67	Robert and Barbara Jackson
69	Jim and Annamarie Nash
71	Alfredo Bautista
73	Tom and Dorothea Rose
75	Tom and Judy Smith
77	Fleaming and Lily Folsom
79	Manuel Salangsang
81	Marthann Conner and son, Charlie
83	Colonel Langdon Harrison
85	Casey and Susan Wnorowski
87	Pat Brody
89	Reason and Lois Warehime
91	Warehime Family
93	Jim and Jean Dennis
95	Jim Dennis
97	Al Maxwell deathbed

Between 1945 and 1960, an estimated 235,000 U.S. servicemen were exposed to nuclear weapons testing during military duty. Almost 1,500 nuclear devices have been detonated since 1945. Approximately 250 of these were American atmospheric nuclear weapons tests. The United States and the Soviet Union stopped surface testing in 1962 due to international pressure, but underground testing continues.

Another estimated 115,000 military personnel were assigned to Hiroshima and Nagasaki and were exposed to the aftermath of the nuclear bombs used at the end of World War II. Still other servicemen were POWs in Japan in the Hiroshima area and witnessed the U.S. use of the atom bomb in war time.

Old photos and films show military personnel in the Nevada desert test sites walking toward the mushroom clouds, through dust and debris, with no protection other than a rifle and a helmet. These men witnessed test series such as Ranger, Buster-Jangle and Tumbler-Snapper. Other servicemen spent their tour of duty on ships or stationed on bases on or near irradiated lagoons in the Pacific. They were ordered deck-top or to the beaches to watch the tests, such as Shots Able and Baker at Operation Crossroads, Shot Wigwam and the 17-shot Redwing series. They slept on the ship decks, exposed to the atmospheric fallout from U.S. tests. They bathed in contaminated lagoon water and sampled the radioactive atmosphere in aircraft.

The men and women who were involved in the testing and use of nuclear weapons while serving in the American military now are known as atomic veterans. This book is a series of portraits and interviews with some of our atomic veterans and their families or survivors. It is their story.

Many of these atomic vets are now profoundly ill and live in expectation of an early death, commonly dying slowly and painfully in their forties and fifties. Many of their children are genetically affected. They and their families have had to bear the emotional and financial costs largely alone. Their government claims the tests did not affect the health of these former servicemen and has refused them compensation or medical help, ruling in most cases they were exposed to no more radiation than they would get in a chest x-ray.

Introduction

X-rays, however, expose tissue to radiation only briefly; a microparticle of plutonium lodged in the body constantly radiates into surrounding tissue. These servicemen lived and worked on contaminated soils, ships and water for extended periods. Plutonium and other radioisotopes could have entered these men's bodies through the air and dust they breathed, the food and water they consumed.

Limited compensation and some medical care has been provided to civilian populations in the Pacific, who are recognized to have extraordinary rates of illness, cancer, premature death, and birth defects as a result of exposure to fallout from American weapons tests. Some $4 billion in claims remain outstanding. Japanese victims of Hiroshima and Nagasaki continue to develop new symptoms and continue to die from their exposure 40 years after the bombing. They too receive limited medical care and some American financial aid. But this help has not been received by the majority of the U.S. atom-

Courtesy of Larry Pray

ic veterans. Why have American atomic veterans and their families found it extraordinarily difficult, if not impossible, to receive assistance from their own country? What made these veterans "immune" to the radiation hazards that so seriously affected the Japanese and the Marshallese?

I first became aware of the atomic veterans in the spring of 1982 through Drs. Susan Lambert and Hank Vyner of the Radiation Research Institute in Berkeley, California. Through them I met Anthony Guarisco, a survivor of the nuclear weapons testing at Bikini Atoll in 1946. He was a 19-year-old sailor then, and a fine athlete. His stories from his tour of duty in Bikini, and his subsequent medical history, stunned me. I hope never to experience the pain he has carried in his body for decades. But it was his eyes that held me. I was to see those eyes over and over again, for most atomic veterans have them. And I had seen them before.

They were the eyes of the Joliot-Curies in a photograph taken in 1947 by Henri Cartier-Bresson. The photograph was in a retrospective of Cartier-Bresson's work I had seen a few years earlier. The photograph held me, perhaps more than any other image in the show. In 1947 the Curies were dying. They were ravaged from the inside as a result of their research with radioactive material. Nothing out of the ordinary showed on the outside except their eyes. They did not look emaciated; their clothes fit. But they lived with death, their bodies filled with pain, with the joints, muscles, bones and soft tissues

Introduction

damaged in extraordinary ways.

Working with atomic veterans has been a visceral confrontation with death, for most of these men know they live under a death sentence in a way most of the rest of us do not. Their bodies betray them, and they feel betrayed. They were and are patriots. They do not understand why they were not told that they would become ill, their bones and muscles and teeth would deteriorate and their immune systems would break down. They wonder why they were not told that they would develop leukemias and rare cancers outside any probable expectations, that they would become old men long before their time, sometimes in their twenties, and that they would not be able to support their families, or even their medical bills. They were not told their children would be born damaged, although some were told not to have children and some had become sterile.

They were sworn to secrecy. They were never to tell anyone, even their families, that they had participated in nuclear weapons testing. And most did stay quiet, and endured the pain and humiliation of their sick bodies. In recent years, a few of them, such as John Burke and Anthony Guarisco and George Seabron, have been speaking out to demand justice—a justice in the form of medical and financial aid for themselves and their families. It is a justice which is still denied.

We need to know the stories of these veterans. They need our help. And we need theirs, for we need to know what they have to teach about how man-made radiation affects living tissue over a period of decades, and how it affects the genetic code. We need to know so that we as individuals and as a society can make informed decisions about our future, so we do not become the blind victims of our own technology.

The atom is unleashed. No matter what is done today we all will be living with man-made radiation for a very long time. And, to a greater or lesser extent, we all have been exposed to radiation—from atmospheric fallout, venting from underground nuclear tests, groundwater contamination, leakage from nuclear waste storage sites, accidents and radiation releases at power plants and reprocessing centers, from uranium mines and their tailings, and the myriad ways radiation enters the environment through human activity. We need to know the truth of the long-term effects of exposure to even low-level ionizing radiation that these men can share with us, if we can listen, see and understand. The time has come for us to understand what these lessons of the Atomic Age mean to each of us personally and what they portend for future generations.

Jim Lerager, 1987

Introduction

Courtesy of Marthann Conner

"Through the release of atomic energy, our generation has brought into the world the most revolutionary force since the prehistoric discovery of fire. This basic power of the universe cannot be fitted into the outmoded concept of narrow nationalisms. For there is no secret and there is no defense; there is no possibility of control except through the aroused understanding and insistence of the peoples of the world.

"We scientists recognize our inescapable responsibility to carry to our fellow citizens an understanding of the simple facts of atomic energy and its implications for society. In this lies our only security and our only hope—we believe that an informed citizenry will act for life and not death."

Albert Einstein, 1947

Introduction

Introduction

Introduction

Introduction

Introduction

THE LONG DEATH

Radiation is like oppression,
the average daily kind of subliminal toothache
you get almost used to, the stench
of chlorine in the water, of smog in the wind.

We comprehend the disasters of the moment,
the nursing home fire, the river in flood
pouring over the sandbag levee, the airplane
crash with fragments of burnt bodies
scattered among the hunks of twisted metal,
the grenade in the marketplace; the sinking ship.

But how to grasp a thing that does not
kill you today or tomorrow
but slowly from the inside in twenty years.
How to feel that a corporate or governmental
choice means we bear twisted genes and our
grandchildren will be stillborn if our
children are very lucky.

Slow death can not be photographed for the six
o'clock news. It's all statistical,
the gross national product or the prime
lending rate. Yet if our eyes saw
in the right spectrum, how it would shine,
lurid as magenta neon.

If we could smell radiation like seeping
gas, if we could sense it as heat, if we
could hear it as a low ominous roar
of the earth shifting, then we would not sit
and be poisoned while industry spokesmen
talk of acceptable millirems and .02
cancer per population thousand.

We acquiesce at murder so long as it is slow,
murder from asbestos dust, from tobacco,
from lead in the water, from sulphur in the air,
and fourteen years later statistics are printed
on the rise in leukemia among children.
We never see their faces. They never stand,
those poisoned children together in a courtyard,
and are gunned down by men in three-piece suits.

The shipyard workers who built nuclear
submarines, the soldiers who were marched
into the Nevada desert to be tested by the
H-bomb, the people who work in power plants,
they die quietly years after in hospital
wards and not on the evening news.

The soft spring rain floats down and the air
is perfumed with pine and earth. Seedlings
drink it in, robins sop it in puddles,
you run in it and feel clean and strong,
the spring rain blowing from the irradiated
cloud over the power plant.

Radiation is oppression, the daily average
kind, the kind you're almost used to
and live with as the years abrade you,
high blood pressure, ulcers, cramps, migraine,
a hacking cough; you take it inside
and it becomes pain and you say, not
They are killing me, but *I am sick now.*

© Marge Piercy from *Circles in the Water*
Reprinted by permission of Alfred A. Knopf, Inc.

Dale and Doris Beaman, son Doug

Dale participated in Operation Crossroads, Bikini Atoll, 1946, as an 18-year-old Navy boiler tender, converting salt water to "fresh" before, during and after tests Able and Baker. Baker was an underwater atomic explosion in the lagoon from which water for the boilers was drawn.

Dale has had colon cancer, kidney surgery, migratory muscle spasms, musculoskeletal deterioration and suffers from diabetes and hypertensive heart disease. Son Doug, 18, has severe musculoskeletal and connective tissue abnormalities. He has had numerous operations, especially to his legs and knees and he is mentally retarded. His condition is deteriorating. Dale's daughters have congenital joint abnormalities.

"I don't recall feeling tired when I went in the service, but I've been tired ever since I was eighteen. I've had a lot of pain over the years and I just took it. I've suffered terrible."

Rudy Florentine, Joanna, Susan and Rudy Jr.

At the end of World War II, Rudy's ship, the USS *Miller*, was ordered to Nagasaki to pick up American prisoners of war. They entered Nagasaki harbor on 7 September 1945. Crew members went on and off the ship, drank and used the local water. The city's reservoir and water supply were contaminated with plutonium from the bomb.

Rudy does not believe he has had an unusual health history. He does have thyroid problems, an enlarged prostate, has had a heart attack and his blood pressure is elevated.

Rudy's wife, Fortunata, comes from a large family. Her seven sisters all have healthy children. Her first two pregnancies, however, ended in miscarriages. Their first surviving child, Joanna, was born in 1960. Joanna's feet turned in, she has had many allergies, has felt tired since childhood and has been hypoglycemic. Joanna is now a physical therapist and has a child. Rudy's second daughter, Susan, was born in 1964, and she seemed fine until she was 15, when she became severely hypoglycemic. She has not been well since. She has become shy and withdrawn. Rudy Jr. was born in 1965. He was born with brain damage. At age two the sutures in his skull closed. They were drilled out and today his skull is wired together. He has nerve disorders, skeletal-muscular development problems, has had many operations and is retarded. He needs constant special attention. The local fire department has made him an honorary fireman and watches out for him.

"I used to wake up at night and say why am I having so much trouble having children?" says Rudy. "It's very depressing that I've had to live my life like this, and my wife, too. I thank God I've got a good wife. I've seen other families with afflicted children break up. . . . We've been married 31 years and we've never had a vacation."

Kay Hinkle, daughters Patti and Holly

Kay's husband, Pat, served in the Navy from 1953 to 1957. In 1956 his ship, a seagoing tug, was assigned to tow target ships and barges to Eniwetok and Bikini Atolls for Operation Redwing.

"They towed in the targets, took sea-depth readings of the target area, then backed away 20 to 40 miles. The targets were blown up. After that, his ship would go right over ground zero, immediately after the blast and take new depth readings. He was exposed to 17 different nuclear explosions over a four-month period," says Kay.

Until 1974, Pat was healthy, although he suffered recurring skin problems, especially on his feet, as well as joint and muscle pain in his back and shoulders. He was hard working, creative and popular. In the fall of 1974 he noticed a swelling in his jaw, which proved to be a malignant tumor. It spread through his neck, shoulder and lymph system. He was operated on three times, in 1975, 1976 and 1980, for the cancer. He recovered quickly from the first two operations, but became increasingly weak. He died from an inoperable brain tumor in February 1981.

Holly was born with a vestigial left hand. All three of Pat and Kay's daughters have spinal alignment problems. Her daughters now have their own healthy children.

"Toward the end, Pat was a bald headed, poor, skinny little thing with a hole in his face, his eye partly sewn closed. It didn't even look anything like Pat. Every evening he'd look up and say, 'I love you so much and I appreciate everything you do.' Cancer's a humiliating, degrading disease. It robs you of everything, your dignity, your intelligence, your pride."

Kay remains an impoverished widow. Her case seeking compensation benefits has been in the courts for five years with no end yet in sight.

Robert and Dorothea Desbien with children Robin, Robert Jr. and Emil

In 1952, Robert Desbien was a young Marine assigned to Operation Tumbler-Snapper in the Nevada desert. He witnessed Shot Dog, a 19-kiloton detonation. Robert was two and a half miles away in a four-foot deep foxhole. The right side of his head was exposed to the flash. He suffered a "severe sunburn," and saw his bones. The troops were frightened and bewildered, the air was full of debris, they were pummeled by the shock and aftershock. Fifteen minutes after detonation they were ordered to ground zero. They reached it 45 minutes after the explosion.

"Our helmet liners and clothing were burning from the fallout. As we marched we were slapping each other to put out the fire. Our feet were burning up. It was like walking on broken glass, the sand crunching under our feet."

They stayed four hours at ground zero, amid blasted equipment and constant fallout. Robert remembers seeing scientists with protective clothing and respirators. And he remembers one scientist crying because he couldn't believe men were out there just totally exposed. When they returned to camp they stripped and showered. Their clothing was taken and burned. Over 1,000 Marines participated in the operation. When Robert later requested his records he was told the men in his operation were exposed to the equivalent of half a dental X-ray.

Robert has had ringing in his right ear since the test and has lost most of his hearing. Since 1969 he has had frequent, crippling muscle spasms. In 1981, one and a half pounds of adhesions were removed from his intestines. Since 1982 he has had open sores on the right side of his face. A biopsy sent to Columbia University indicated the cause was radiation exposure. He has a pre-cataract condition. He is under medication to control chronic pain. In 1981 the family almost lost their home. Robert currently works two jobs to pay his bills.

"A couple years ago when we really felt Dad was going to die, we were so scared," says Robin. "He is very hopeful, a strong-willed man, a dreamer, a hard worker, very ambitious, an inventor. . . . He loves his country, but he is very bitter. He can't understand how the government did such an awful thing to so many people and can deny every bit of it."

Joan McCarthy

Tom McCarthy, Joan's husband, died in April 1981. In 1955, as a 19-year-old sailor, he had participated in Operation Wigwam, an underwater nuclear detonation off the coast of Mexico, 500 miles from San Diego. Tom said a plume of water rose 2,000 feet in the air. The water churned and washed over the ships. His ship was five miles from ground zero. During the week the ship remained in the test area many men reported to sick bay. Men doubled over with cramps.

Joan learned later that very high radiation levels were reported from San Diego to San Francisco at the time of this test. The governor of California is reported to have been dissuaded from declaring a state of emergency by federal and military officials. The test area was declared an underwater desert, devoid of life. Joan remembers Tom saying the purpose of the operation was to test the effect on the equipment and marine life. Joan asks, "But what about the men?"

After the Navy, Tom became a very successful transportation planner. In his mid-thirties he started experiencing debilitating muscle spasms, joint problems and severe skin rashes. He looked old. He became disoriented, had memory lapses and blackouts. When he was 39, he lost his job. Tom was stoic about his pain and problems and worked odd jobs when he could, but they lost their home and lived largely on savings. The family experienced tremendous financial and emotional pressures. When Tom died, his body was riddled with cancer. There were holes in his bones. He looked like he was 80. Joan has since raised their three children on social security income.

Joan has talked to a number of crew members from Tom's ship, all of whom have had cancer. She now counsels atomic veterans and their families.

"Towards the end all Tom was praying for was peace. No one should live that kind of horror. . . . I never accepted the fact that he could die. He was young and we had plans and goals. The government should recognize there is a problem, not to incur blame, but to acknowledge and be responsible for what has happened. What happened to the veterans is happening to more and more people on a global scale."

Herman and Elva Tinsley

Colonel Tinsley served in the Air Force from 1942 to 1971. He witnessed two nuclear explosions at Christmas Island in 1962. He was a pilot flying reconnaissance missions.

"I was in the airplane sampling air on numerous, foreign and domestic nuclear testing, collecting air samples. We flew through the aftermath of the explosion to see how dirty it was."

Colonel Tinsley had the first of numerous skin cancer operations in 1968. He had an operation for fibrous sarcoma of the right leg in 1978. This cancer recurred and his right leg was removed at the hip socket. He has had a chronic skin rash since 1965. He lives with continual pain and is extremely sensitive to light.

"One of my navigators passed away and it was a leg-type cancer. He passed away 11 years ago in his mid-forties. He was about my age."

Frank, Marcia, Tim and Margaret Pazel

Frank was in the Army, assigned to Eniwetok from March 1956 to April 1957. He remembers witnessing about a dozen tests from May to July 1956. The tests ranged in size and type from a small tactical weapon seven miles away to the most spectacular test Frank witnessed, an underwater shot in the lagoon, which sent a column of water thousands of feet in the air "topped by a cloud with a ghoulish purple glow."

As the testing approached, the population of the island increased from 2,000 to 10,000. All the troops were ordered to witness each test. During the testing Frank remembers there was general anxiety among the troops, doubts about the scientists, discussions of the moral issues.

"A couple of times when there were unexpected windshifts, the south end of the island got very heavy dosages according to the radiation safety monitoring team. One of my roommates was on the team. 'What if the bastards had miscalculated?' we wondered. The last test was a large hydrogen bomb detonated in the predawn hours at Bikini Atoll. From 185 miles away it lit up the whole sky like high noon. The shock wave at Eniwetok was so powerful it caused panic."

While on the island Frank developed a painful rash over his entire body. He had no health problems until he discovered a large mole on his lower back in the fall of 1983. He underwent extensive surgery in December 1983 for malignant melanoma. In April 1984 the melanoma reappeared in his groin. He had his second operation. A third operation in August 1984 showed no new disease.

"Statistically I have a 40 percent chance to live five years. That vision of death with his scepter is in front of me. The government has an immense responsibility to admit there is a high causal relationship [between test exposure and the physical problems of veterans], an immense responsibility to do something . . . I don't think they can cop out by saying the decision to expose military personnel was made by some guy 25 years ago."

Frank's melanoma recurred. He died in February 1986.

George and Rita Seabron

George was a sailor at Bikini Atoll in 1946 during tests Able and Baker. He later spent several months "decontaminating" ships from those tests. His ship also transported other military personnel back from Bikini to the United States, many of whom were very sick.

"We were told they were seasick. I thought it was weird. They came off of ships, why were they seasick?"

George believes some ships were sold to other countries and private companies. "They dragged back target ships to Hunter's Point, [in San Francisco Bay where they tried to] decontaminate them in dry dock and [finally] took them to the Farallons and sunk them. How many people were exposed aboard those ships? Civilians, who didn't know!"

George developed headaches, rashes, dizziness. He has stomach problems which continue today. Debilitating back, bone and muscle problems began in 1952. He is sterile.

"I'm constantly in pain. Each year it gets worse, [but] I never quit working. That's what keeps me going."

George's health is deteriorating. He had a heart attack in 1986. His blood tests reveal abnormalities now and his condition may point to the onset of leukemia.

Walter Hooke

Walter was a Marine Corps lieutenant assigned to Nagasaki from October 1945 to February 1946. After his military service, he became the senior vice president of United Parcel Service in charge of personnel. He is now retired.

About Nagasaki he recalls: "The damage wasn't so shocking as was the appearance of the people, the various types and degrees of burns." Much of Walter's time was spent touring the city by jeep. He met and befriended the Catholic bishop of Nagasaki. Through him Walter met Japanese doctors, teachers and professionals. Over the years he has read extensively about the issues and results of atomic testing.

"Starting in the Pacific in 1946 from Operation Crossroads on, military personnel were exposed to dangers that were known and kept from the people involved. The Atomic Energy Commission was reluctant to let the military engage in the tests in the first place. This has been documented. The military more or less said they wouldn't participate unless they could put the troops in relatively close ranges, much closer than the AEC recognized as being safe. . . . You read how quickly they made financial settlements with Japanese fishermen [the fishing boat Lucky Dragon, contaminated by fallout in 1954], moved people off [fallout-contaminated] Micronesian islands and replaced all the topsoil. They know there is a serious problem. But because of jeopardizing their entire nuclear program they won't admit any possibility of exposure to the veterans who took part in those tests.

"After having talked to close to a hundred of these atomic veterans who have had serious effects, or their relatives and survivors, I know the position of the government is to deny any connection [between radiation exposure and illness]. When you talk to some of the really patriotic veterans, they are hurt more than some of the rest of us because they can't believe their government would ever do anything to them like this. . . . Most are a lot younger than I, they had their exposure at Crossroads in 1946, on into the late 1950s and early 1960s and they have terrible problems, both themselves and their children."

Don and Margaret Cordray

Don was a 19-year-old sailor at the two atomic tests at Bikini Atoll in 1946. In the 1950s he set up accountability systems at a top secret nuclear weapons storage and testing facility near Lake Mead, Nevada.

Don first experienced dizziness and back, leg and internal pain in the 1950s. He suffered chronic skin rashes, arthritis, bone deterioration, tooth loss, gastrointestinal problems and constant, severe pain. He had a kidney operation in 1974 and an intestinal operation in 1975. In 1976 he was diagnosed as having oat cell cancer, a virulent cancer which spreads rapidly throughout the body. The cancer was brought under control, but the medical bill totaled $200,000.

"I figured [at the time of service] the government was giving us protection at Bikini, but two senior Navy officers made the statement that they advised against the tests due to what it would do to human health."

The statement Don refers to was made prior to the 1946 Bikini tests. He found the statement while researching Operation Crossroads and his own exposure.

Don was very successful in the Navy and later in private business and therefore had the resources to pay for his expensive medical treatment.

"I think there's so much sadness that the government can ignore the atomic veterans. I'm more fortunate [financially] than most. They're living by the skin of their teeth. But I'm experiencing physical problems along with the others. More problems come, different surgeries, eventually cancer, disablement, death."

Don died in February 1984 at the age of 56. He looked and moved like a man of 80.

Bill and Jane Dolan, daughter Nancy

Bill was assigned to Operation Ivy, Eniwetok Atoll, in 1952. He witnessed two tests. On 1 November 1952, Shot Mike, the world's first hydrogen device, was detonated. Its explosive force measured 10.4 megatons, still one of the most powerful nuclear devices ever exploded. Fifteen days later, Shot King was detonated. It was a 500-kiloton, plutonium-based atomic bomb, the largest ever of its type.

All Eniwetok personnel were evacuated to ships for Shot Mike. Bill witnessed the blast from the deck of a ship 17 miles away. He felt extreme heat, then the loudest sound he has ever heard. Within an hour the cloud measured 100 miles in circumference. Ocean water was drawn 10,000 feet into the atmosphere. The next day they returned to Eniwetok. They had covered their personal gear with canvas before leaving the island. The canvas was heavily contaminated, was taken away and burned. No other safety precautions were taken and men got sick.

On November 16, Shot King was dropped from a B-36 bomber. The troops were lined up on the island with their backs to the lagoon, four and a half miles from ground zero. Twenty minutes after the detonation it rained. Bill had returned to his tent, but most personnel were caught outside. Since 1979 he has talked to 115 other veterans of Ivy.

"Anyone who was out in that rain, frolicking, has some kind of medical problem, mostly a skin cancer type problem, plus hearing, sight and other disorders. The rain came from the atomic cloud that drifted over the island. . . . Two [of the Ivy survivors Bill talked to] were physicists. They were very upset about that rainfall."

Bill has lost most of his teeth and his gums are chronically infected. Nancy reports he has been in pain for the last few years. He has stomach and kidney problems. Bill feels he is one of the lucky ones—that his health has mostly been good. Daughter Nancy had a normal childhood, but is increasingly ill. Her immune system is failing.

"Nobody realizes the tragedy that is going on with these atomic veterans," says Jane. "A lot of people feel they are making up these stories. But you have thousands of veterans with cases and cases that you know aren't normal."

Chelo Amaro

A member of the U.S. Air Force from 1943 to 1946, Chelo maintained and operated heavy earth-moving equipment. He was stationed in Hiroshima from August to December 1945, operating trucks and bulldozers from ground zero to a radius of 17 miles. He was 22 years old at the time. He has felt chronically tired since December 1945.

After World War II, Chelo worked as a master diesel mechanic. He has had chronic gastrointestinal and colon problems since the early 1950s and has undergone numerous operations. He developed skin problems in the early 1960s. He has been unable to work since 1979 because of extreme swelling, cracking and fissuring of his hands. He has lost his home and savings.

"I made a lot of money but it seems like it's always been doctors, doctors, doctors. I had a home and we ate good and I should have had good money but you can't when you are all the time fighting doctors."

His daughter was born with severe musculoskeletal abnormalities and suffered chronic internal problems throughout childhood. She completed college, but died in her early twenties.

Chelo has become increasingly ill and destitute. He still focuses on his major goal in life—living to age 80.

Donald Rutan, daughter Wendy

Donald was born in 1943. In 1962 he was on board the USS *Norton Sound*, assigned to Operation Dominic for six weeks. He remembers watching the fireballs from nuclear tests. While in the Pacific, he developed white blisters over his upper torso. Six months later he reported to sick bay, and was diagnosed with skin cancer. He had about 200 skin growths removed while in the Navy. Since then he has had another 2,000 removed.

Donald also suffers from hypertension, cysts in his jaws, increasing cramping and pain in his arms, legs and back. Feeling weak and fatigued, he says, "I can't get out of my own way." His teeth are disintegrating. He has debilitating rashes on his hands and feet and he is sensitive to light. He has three teenage children, all of whom have had complicated medical histories. Donald has had a difficult work history because of his medical problems and has had high medical bills.

"Since I was little he would always go to Buffalo or New Jersey for weeks for medical treatment," says daughter Wendy. "We just try to keep going ahead and not backwards."

Donald feels he wouldn't have become so sick if he hadn't been exposed to radiation as a child. He played in an area where uranium mine tailings were dumped. Houses have now been built on the site.

"Radiation is bad, the way they handle and treat it. Either evolution has to resolve the problem or everyone will be poisoned to death."

Anthony and Mary Guarisco

Anthony witnessed Operation Crossroads, tests Able and Baker at Bikini Atoll in 1946, when he was 19. He was hospitalized at Bikini for what was labeled "severe influenza." He has had chronic physical problems since 1946 including recurring week-long bouts of "flu," progressive musculoskeletal deterioration and nerve, lung, bladder, prostate and testicular problems. Anthony had to retire from his career as a plumber in his mid-forties because of his health. He had a temporary bout of blindness in his twenties and his vision and hearing are deteriorating.

Anthony's son and daughter have urological problems similar to his. A grandson was born with a life-threatening growth in his middle ear.

"I've always had pain. I live with pain 24 hours a day. I've been in pain every day for the last 30 years. I feel bad about my children suffering from something they may be deriving from myself."

Geri Spang and Jeff McAllister

As an 18-year-old Marine, Jim McAllister was assigned to the Nevada desert to participate in Teapot Series, Shot Bee, 22 March 1955. The men were in trenches at 3,000 meters. Bee was an incomplete detonation and the men were covered with black, radioactive soot. They performed battlefield maneuvers, then left the area.

Within a year Jim became chronically ill, although his health had been perfect as a child. He began to suffer allergies, frequent colds, depression, dental problems, later neurological symptoms including paralysis in his hands and legs and blackouts. His hearing failed and he suffered temporary blindness and blurred vision. He was discharged from the military for "personality disorders" in 1960. As time went on he developed growths and tumors. Just before he died, he said, "Things are growing in my body like little flowers." He died 14 October 1983.

At his death, his sister, Geri Spang, became the guardian for his son, Jeff.

"He was extremely proud to be a Marine. He received a Presidential Citation," says Geri. "But he was ridiculed by the Veterans Administration doctors for being concerned about the growths. They called him a hypochondriac. I encouraged him to go to other doctors. He said, 'The VA doctors are the finest on earth.' Some of the VA doctors truly saw there was a problem, but the treatment he received was cruel, callous and immoral."

"We would work together around the house," remembers Jeff of his father. "But he was tired all the time and would have to lay down. I knew he was a Marine. I wanted to be a Marine just like him. We played All American Kids. We were the Yankees, we'd go off to fight the Russians. Me and my dad just thought he had an ulcer problem, just like the VA doctor said.

"I feel the government has been pulling a bunch of tricks on us. I don't want to be a Marine anymore."

Geri has been trying without success to get benefits for Jeff since Jim's death.

Al and Jackie Maxwell

Al joined the Army in 1939, was sent to the Philippines in 1940 and was taken prisoner by the Japanese at Bataan. He survived death marches and slave labor camps. He was among a contingent of POWs laboring in a steel mill near Hiroshima on 6 August 1945.

"We were aware of a large explosion which lit up the sky. Dark clouds came over us and a dirty rain. . . . Fifteen of us were sent on work details into Hiroshima, sent in to clean up debris. We saw the devastation, could see the white outline of bodies. . . . We developed rashes anywhere skin was bare."

Al has gastrointestinal problems and lives with chronic pain. He has severe muscle spasms. In 1981 he was diagnosed with and treated for multiple myeloma, leukemia of the bone marrow. He has had ribs crack just from sneezing.

Al and Jackie are Mormons. Both come from very large, healthy, long-lived families. They were determined to have children. Jackie had six pregnancies, beginning in 1948. One pregnancy did not come to term. The fetus was badly malformed. Two births seemed normal, but the babies died within 36 hours from lung complications. Two babies were born hydrocephalic and with all four heart chambers defective. One lived 15 months, the other five years. After the first two pregnancies, doctors asked Jackie repeatedly if she had been exposed to radiation. Finally one doctor questioned Al, and Al told him about being in Hiroshima. (He had not told Jackie.) This doctor had had three colleagues who worked in early radiation studies and all three had died. They had had children with genetic defects. He advised Al and Jackie not to try for more children. Al and Jackie have one normal child from Jackie's fourth pregnancy. Their daughter now has two healthy children.

Al entered the hospital for the last time in June 1986. He died after a prolonged struggle on 21 February 1987.

Jackie works part time and is dependent on the charity of relatives. She still seeks benefits, but has been told by the Veterans Administration her husband died of pneumonia.

Tim Nuzum

Tim joined the Navy in 1961. He was sent to Christmas Island for test series Dominic in 1962.

"I was 19 years old. I didn't think too much about radiation hazards. We never had any training as to the dangers of it. Some of the tests were dropped from B-52s, some were underwater torpedoes or mine fields, that kind of thing.

"Up until now, I feel lucky I don't have some form of cancer or other related disease. It's been 20 years now. If they are going to occur, they'll be starting to show up now.

"We thought we were doing the patriotic thing. But now that I think back on it and hear about all those terrible things people in former tests have gone through, I think it would have been more patriotic to protest."

Ben and Patricia Fudge

Ben was an Army mechanic assigned to Eniwetok in 1955. He was present for the Castle series of nuclear tests and was mustered out on the beach to witness each test. After Shot Bravo, the island was almost evacuated because of high radiation levels. Ben did lots of fishing, swimming, water skiing and snorkeling, especially around the old Japanese and American shipwrecks in the atoll.

In 1956 he developed a rash on his arms and legs that looked like cold sores. The rash reappeared seasonally for about ten years. Since 1971 his teeth and gums have been disintegrating; his gums are chronically infected. His thyroid gland had completely disintegrated by 1975, but his thyroid level is kept in balance with medication. He feels fortunate that he has always had access to superb medical facilities through his job. Today he feels fine and is physically very active, but he worries about his children. Both his son and daughter have progressive back and muscle problems and pain.

"I'd like to see the government acknowledge there is a problem, and give medical care to the veterans and their children. You cannot sue the government, a veteran like myself cannot sue the government because of the Ferres Doctrine. I love the work I do [for a defense contractor] and feel it is very important, but I am an atomic veteran also and work on systems that deliver atomic weapons. Should I give up my job? I just can't walk out of a job like that. I like my job and it is my whole financial livelihood. What should I do?"

Barry and Betty Kail

Barry was in the Navy. He participated in Operation Hardtack, a 4.2-megaton bomb detonated at 250,000 feet over the Pacific the night of 31 July 1958. Since 1958 Barry has had chronic itching, swelling and cracking of the hands, feet, groin and torso. He suffers chronic fatigue and debilitating pain, joint and bone problems, severe bronchial and gastrointestinal problems, and bleeding from the rectum. He is now unable to work. Betty says, "His feet swell, crack and bleed. He would come home with his shoes full of blood." His children have some similar symptoms, though less severe.

"My first physical problems manifested within one year. Some people's problems are manifesting 20 to 25 years later—the most dreaded, cancer. That's the fear of every atomic veteran, that we're all just survivors for the moment."

Larry Pray, mother Helen

Larry joined the Marines in 1951. In 1952 he was assigned to Camp Mercury at the Nevada test site. Larry witnessed Tumbler-Snapper D, a 19-kiloton bomb dropped from a plane. His outfit was assigned to trenches 7,000 yards from ground zero. Equipment and material was placed in concentric rings every 500 yards from the blast center.

"I'm sure glad it's an offensive weapon, because there's no defense against it," Larry remembers thinking at the time. "When it went off there was smoke and fire, it seemed like they were probably moving hell and taking the first load through. . . . The fireball rose 25,000 to 30,000 feet. There was a pressure wave.

"We marched on ground zero immediately. They said, 'No danger.' There was a tank. Its side was melted. We inspected the site and observed the equipment. . . . We were swept with a broom, checked with a Geiger counter. There were wind and dust storms while we were there. Then we returned to California and forgot all about it."

Larry had severe headaches between 1954 and 1957. By 1959, when he was 28, his gums were bleeding and teeth were loose. Teeth and gum problems have persisted. In 1961 Larry was operated on for a brain tumor. The tumor was successfully removed, but Larry remains partially paralyzed.

Harvey and Margaret Kokka, son Ken

Harvey was in the Army Signal Corps from 1954 to 1957. He was stationed on Eniwetok Island for 13 months and participated in Operation Redwing. An atomic device was detonated on the atoll during his tour.

"We figured the Army knew what it was doing and wouldn't endanger us. I visited one of the islands where they did some tests years and years before. There was practically nothing growing on the island."

Harvey had an operation for colon cancer in 1977. He is experiencing progressive, involuntary twisting of the neck, cramping of the hand, vision deterioration, skin growths on his face and increasing difficulties at work from physical ailments.

"A year ago I could control the cramping mentally. I can't today. I still wait for the other shoe to drop. I think of these other vets and I think, 'Jesus Christ, is something like that going to come to me, and if so how will I deal with it?'"

Burney Durkin

In 1951 Burney was a sailor aboard the USS *Curtis*, the command ship for Operation Greenhouse. The *Curtis* carried the bombs and scientists to Eniwetok Atoll for the test series. At first Burney was glad to be out of the cold and wet of Korea. He was present for four nuclear tests. He was on deck for the tests and could see the bones in his hands and arms when the bombs went off.

"We were nine to thirteen miles from the blast and moving toward ground zero. I was a member of the decontamination crew after the blasts, washing the decks down with water and scrubbing them with sand and stone, and we did that while barefoot and without any protective equipment. [The rest of the crew was kept below decks] . . . . We were contaminated with fallout. I have a picture of a Marshallese girl after Shot Bravo in 1954 and she had beta burns [from fallout]. That was identical to the way my neck and shoulder looked in 1951. The other members of the deck crew also had burns."

Burney was a high school athlete. Since age 20 he has been chronically tired and weak. Persistent fevers and night sweats began in 1965. In 1966 he was hospitalized with lymphoma cancer. The treatments were debilitating, and for some time Burney could not support his family. He had four young children.

Since 1966 Burney has experienced increasing pain, although his lymphoma remains in remission. He has had thyroid abnormalities since 1975. In 1984 three malignant basal cell cancers were removed. In 1983 his 24-year-old son died from Hodgkin's disease, a form of leukemia.

"I'm just one of the thousands of victims of the biggest whitewash since Tom Sawyer painted Aunt Polly's fence. We're still the greatest country in the world. We produced some good men, the veterans, but unfortunately we've abandoned them and that's a disgrace. Evil persists because good men do nothing."

Leon Walker

Leon was at Operation Crossroads in 1946. He was in the Navy and was ordered on deck for both tests Able and Baker.

"I saw through my eyelids and arm. I turned around in time to see a [target] ship actually out of the water in a vertical position. We were that close."

The ship that was lifted vertically out of the water was the battleship *Alabama*. Navy photographs corroborate Leon's statement.

Leon was among the sailors ordered aboard the aircraft carrier *Saratoga*, one of the target ships, after the detonations. He and many other men from his ship became sick at Bikini. "I suffered severe headaches, nausea, weariness and an aching feeling I'd never had before." He and many other men also developed skin rashes at Bikini and what they were told was "seasickness."

He had a heart attack/stroke approximately four years after the test, while still in his early twenties. His disabilities have prevented him from holding steady employment and he survives on welfare. He remains partially paralyzed on his left side and on crutches. He has hypertension and heart disease.

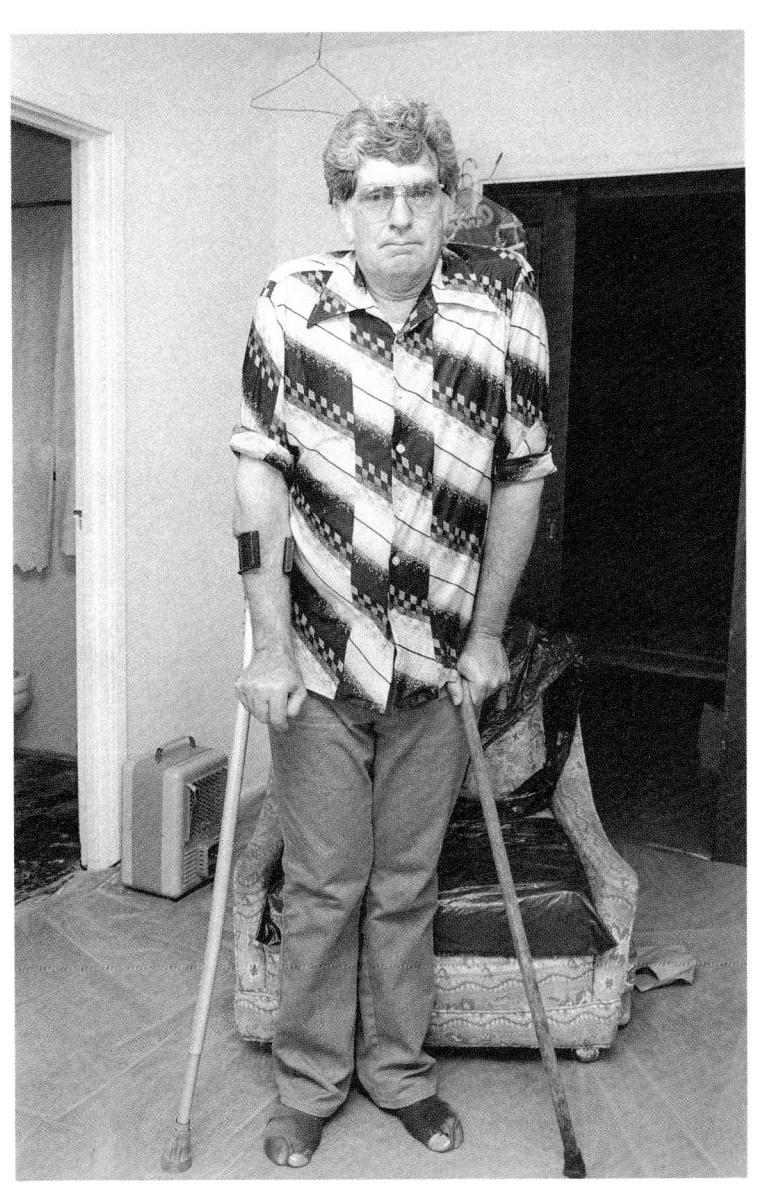

John Delay

John was drafted into the Army in 1956. He was assigned to the Eniwetok atomic testing ground in February 1957. He was given a security clearance after a thorough background check, but was not given any training or warnings about exposure to radiation. John was told never to discuss the testing under threat of prosecution for treason. He did not tell even his family about it until 1982, after reading articles about atomic veterans.

John remembers three or four tests spaced at two- to three-day intervals. He witnessed the tests from the beach and was told there would be no effects from exposure. A few weeks after the tests John developed large boils on his face.

John worked in the base laundry. He believes he may have handled contaminated clothing. He lived in tents for his year on Eniwetok. It rained almost every day. Movies were shown at night, outdoors, even in the rain. The men were told not to eat coconuts and bananas from surrounding islands, but were never warned against swimming and collecting shells.

John has problems with his joints and bones. He lives with a dull aching in his bones most of the time and has restricted mobility. He has medically verified chromosome damage. All three of his children have severe allergies and respiratory problems. His 17-year-old daughter suffers from a condition which has required traveling to New York City for treatment and injections every month since she was three.

"They had the gall to use us as guinea pigs when they knew from the Manhattan project and the first testing in the Pacific there was going to be damage. We now know from the Warren papers [Colonel Stafford Warren was the chief of radiation safety at the Bikini Island tests in 1946] that they knew all along about health effects and they still went ahead and did it."

Robert Campbell

Robert was an Army personnel specialist stationed on Eniwetok from October 1950 to November 1951. He and 10,000 other men, civilian and military, participated in Operation Greenhouse, a four-shot test series including an early hydrogen blast.

Robert witnessed the tests from the edge of the lagoon. Shot Dog, the hydrogen test, was 27 miles away. At that distance, with his back to the blast and his eyes covered, he could still see the bones in his arms. After each test the men would go to breakfast.

"The mess hall is immediately adjacent to the runway. The drone planes are flown through the nuclear cloud. They would land, then taxi and back up in front of the mess hall and offload the test equipment. . . . The planes have not been washed down. They are as hot as hell so that's what you get for your breakfast."

Robert says fallout smells like burning flesh. Shot Item, a 500-kiloton blast, created four days of fallout on the island. Navy personnel on ships were confined below decks, but the men on the island carried on normal duty dressed in shirts and shorts.

Robert has had recurring rashes on his back since 1951. The skin on his feet cracks and bleeds. Growths were removed from his stomach and intestines and he has rectal spasms. In 1954 all his teeth were extracted. He had bouts of blindness in 1954 and 1956 and remains sensitive to light. He had two acute miocardial infarctions at age 39 and a mild stroke in 1981. His daughter died of leukemia at age 12. Three other pregnancies ended in miscarriages. He has no living children.

"You get tired of being sick. You have to fight being tired. You live with chronic pain . . . I have plutonium, cesium, strontium in me. Basically what it means is one day it's going to become one cellular insult too many and I'm going to die of cancer."

Donna Smith-Harrison and husband, Sam

Donna's father, Donald Smith, worked in nuclear security for the Air Force and private contractors. Between 1953 and 1961, he attended five series of nuclear tests.

He began passing kidney stones in 1955. In the 1960s he developed bursitis and had two kidney operations. He survived an operation for colon cancer in 1975, but was diagnosed with liver cancer in 1979. He was then serving as chief of nuclear security for Oak Ridge National Laboratories. He died in 1981.

"My father was a real patriot. He really loved the military. When he was dying it was really hard for him to cope with the idea that his life's work was causing his death."

Jim, Barrie, Kelly and Kevin Benson

From March to October 1956, Jim served as an assistant historian for the Air Force weather service. Jim witnessed 12 tests at Eniwetok. The aircraft of Jim's group left Eniwetok immediately after each detonation, returning to the island four days later.

"It was really beautiful. It was gorgeous the way it lit up the whole [night] sky. The skies lit up and stayed lit for a good five to ten minutes."

Jim enjoys good health. He did not give his experience at Eniwetok much thought until 1980 when he answered an advertisement in the paper seeking atomic veterans.

"I thought I might meet some of my old friends from over there. I went to one meeting at Rutgers University. I couldn't go back. I felt sick listening to all these people. I felt so bad for them I couldn't handle it anymore. The people [atomic veterans at Rutgers] got up and talked about themselves having cancer or the wives talked about their deceased husbands and how they died and how they agonized before they died and how the government didn't do anything and they had to go mostly to private doctors. Some tried to sue the government and nothing happened. Some brought their [chronically ill or genetically abnormal] children and said this is the result [of exposure], but the government said it has never been proven that it is a direct result of any kind of atomic radiation. . . . I figured I might see some old friends I hadn't seen in 20 years, but what I came back with was a horrible experience."

"I can't believe the government would allow these things to happen," adds Barrie. "And once they did, to not acknowledge it at all!"

Robert and Barbara Jackson

While in the Navy, Robert participated in Operation Dominic at Christmas Island in 1962. It was the last series of American atmospheric nuclear weapons tests, just prior to the Nuclear Test Ban Treaty. Robert remembers approximately 13 nuclear detonations while he was at Christmas Island. He believes there were another ten to 15 after he left. To date, he is in good health.

"My impression at the time was how pretty it was. The effects years later on people are ridiculous. It may even end humanity. We've got to get people's attention."

"Before he told me, I didn't know anything about it," adds Barbara. "I thought they shot off bombs at Hiroshima and Nagasaki and that was it. When I told my mother about [Bob's exposure], she asked, 'Can you catch it?' There's a lot of ignorance out there."

Jim and Annamarie Nash

Jim is now a high school principal. In June and July of 1957 he was a young Marine Corps officer assigned to Camp Desert Rock, Nevada. He witnessed Shot Hood, the largest nuclear device tested in the United States. It was estimated to be between 75 and 78 kilotons.

"All the experts the Marine Corps brought in maintained there was no possible harm that could come to us, no short- or long-term consequences."

A large number of troops witnessed Hood. Jim's outfit was assigned to trenches 4,500 yards from ground zero. When the bomb went off the trenches partially collapsed, sending dust and debris everywhere. After 45 minutes Jim's outfit was transported by truck to ground zero. Other troops advanced by helicopter and on foot. Everything within 1,000 yards was vaporized. The ground crunched like glass underfoot. Ash fell constantly on the men, burning skin and clothing. Jim saw Atomic Energy Commission personnel wearing protective suits and respirators. They came into the test area, took their readings and left quickly. The bomb was exploded at 4:40 a.m. The troops remained on site until late morning. They were brushed down with brooms.

Jim had cysts removed from his neck in the 1950s and 1960s. He has had a hyperthyroid condition since the mid-1960s and has hypertension. In 1981 the skin peeled off his hands and feet.

Jim has studied the history of the nuclear testing program. Testing began in Nevada in the early 1950s. A very large number of tests were conducted in 1957 and 1958.

"The soil [at Camp Desert Rock] is filled with radioactive emitters. You walked and slept on that soil. Scientists have said anybody who lived and slept on that soil for a two- to six-week period—their expression is, 'Those guys were fried.' [In 1957 and 1958] San Francisco had very high radiation levels. Los Angeles and Salt Lake City were ridiculous. The Surgeon General is reported to have told the President's Council of Scientific Advisors that in no way could they release the statistics that would inform the citizenry of Los Angeles of the amount of radiation they were exposed to because it would create a national panic. The testing program was a joke because they had a ready made control group [the atomic veterans] by which they could measure the effect of radiation, and they were not interested in finding out what those effects were. At best it was very poor science, at worst it was criminal."

Alfredo Bautista

Alfredo served in the Philippines Scouts in World War II, then in the U. S. Army. He was assigned to Camp Desert Rock, Nevada, for a nuclear weapon test in 1951.

"When the bomb exploded it got hot—too hot. [I was temporarily] blinded. My ears were ringing. I could see through my hands. None of the soldiers were in trenches. The civilian scientists were further away in bunkers. We walked to ground zero after maybe 15 minutes."

He was not allowed to wash, clean up or change clothing until he returned to California two or three days after the detonation. His protection was a helmet and an overcoat.

"When I retired I was getting weak. I was still a young man. I didn't plan to retire, but I started getting weak. [After retiring] I started feeling everything."

Alfredo has suffered increasingly debilitating health problems since 1954, beginning with chronic tiredness and itchy skin. In the late 1950s he lost his teeth, and developed arthritis in his back, joints and hands. He has high blood pressure and heart problems and has been unable to work since 1973.

Tom and Dorothea Rose

Tom was a 19-year-old sailor aboard the USS *Renville* in 1958. His ship was assigned to Operation Hardtack II, at Eniwetok Atoll. He witnessed several tests.

"We wanted to see it, the mushroom clouds. We heard all the noise. The waves would sweep across the bay and all of the ships would jump all over. There were target ships and they were brought back, sometimes tied next to other ships."

Tom's health has remained good. In about 1980, he began to meet other atomic veterans. He remembers fellow veteran Tom Smith, in particular, who was also at Hardtack.

"He [Tom Smith] was in bad shape and he had one complication after another. He's the guy who could die one of these days. He is a youthful looking person. He lives in a middle class house, but that's where it all stops. I met him. It's just too painful to think all of a sudden I could be like Tom Smith.

"I think sometimes people don't want to hear about it because it's too painful. I think in general people don't want to know about poverty, about nuclear war, nuclear waste, chemicals and garbage in the food we eat, because if you really start thinking about those things you may have to live your life a little differently.

"When I was growing up I didn't know anybody who didn't want to go in the military. These atomic veterans are so much like other veterans. They love their country so much."

Tom and Judy Smith

Tom Smith was a 19-year-old sailor assigned to Operation Hardtack, Eniwetok Atoll, in the spring of 1958. His ship was a tender for four target vessels. He witnessed approximately 15 blasts. He remembers seeing ground zero and the target vessels clearly from his duty station. Within a few days of each test, the target vessels were towed back and tied up to Tom's vessel. He and the other members of his crew routinely boarded the targets, installing and removing monitoring equipment.

On two occasions his ship was so contaminated that most of the crew was confined below decks with all doors sealed. Both times Tom was assigned topside to the decontamination team. They washed the ship down with scrub brushes and seawater. They wore T-shirts and dungarees.

"Standing out there when the heat flash hit would make your dungarees so hot they would almost burn you. [After an underwater test,] the masts were jumping around like they were going to break. It felt like the ship was coming apart. The officers said we were way too close."

Tom was an athlete and outdoorsman and stayed in top condition until the mid-1960s. He first suffered gastritis and diarrhea at Eniwetok, and gastrointestinal problems have persisted. He suffers hearing loss and thyroid problems. He has nerve damage, night sweats and chronic, debilitating pain. He had an excellent work history until 1975, then long periods of disability. He has been unable to work since 1980. He had excellent medical insurance, and Judy now works, so they have survived financially.

Judy and Tom have two children, Jason and Jonna. Both were hyperactive and learning disabled when they were young. At 19, Jason's spine is deteriorating. He has scoliosis. Jonna's hips are rotated and she has bone abnormalities.

"They called us volunteers. We volunteered for service but not for Eniwetok. What really upsets me now is they won't own up and won't stand by what they did. I'm not going to live to die of old age. I doubt that very seriously."

Fleaming and Lily Folsom

In 1947 and 1948, Fleaming was a Navy lab technician working with plutonium extracts from Operation Crossroads. Fleaming also went aboard target vessels to scrape samples for analysis. He and other technicians handled radioactive materials without gloves and pipetted with mouth pipettes. He got plutonium extracts in his mouth, would spit and wash it out. He was hospitalized at this time for several weeks with strong stomach pains. In the lab, mice were injected with radioactive materials, and human experiments with prisoners were discussed and prepared for, although not carried out to Fleaming's knowledge. A civilian woman washed contaminated glassware.

In 1950 and 1951 he was assigned to Japtan Island, Eniwetok Atoll to conduct animal experiments. He witnessed three tests, one from a distance of 2.5 miles. The heat was terrific and all he could see were the bones of his arms, legs and torso. He recalls thinking: "What the hell's happened to me? I'm nothing but a skeleton! If I could invent an X-ray that would show up so well I'd be a millionaire in a month."

After a rain shower, all the monitors went off scale. "It was hotter on our home island (Japtan) than the test island." Higher authorities were contacted, but the crew was not removed.

In 1962 his vision began to deteriorate and he lost peripheral vision. He is now nearly blind. He has had internal bleeding and a stroke. His spine and joints have been deteriorating. He blacks out and has fallen many times. He can no longer lift anything. His jaw is full of puss. He says: "Every bone in my body hurts."

His son is hypersensitive, grew extra teeth in his mouth and had constant orthodontic work from age six to 14. Both Fleaming and Lily had perfect teeth.

A friend of Fleaming's, Allan Nelson, had been with him at Eniwetok. He was hospitalized in the mid-1970s and, recalls Fleaming, "The doctors wanted to know if he had been around radiation. Two weeks after he was hospitalized he died. He died six or eight years ago."

"It was a real nightmare with both of them [Fleaming and their son] sick," says Lily. "Most all those people are going to die of cancer. One way or another it's going to eat them up."

**Manuel Salangsang
speaking about his father, Adriano**

Adriano Salangsang entered the Army in 1931. He was stationed at the Atomic Warfare Training Center, Camp Desert Rock, Nevada, during the summers of 1954, 1955 and 1956. His son, Manuel, remembers his father's service to the U.S. military.

"There were at times six to a dozen [nuclear] detonations a day. He was right in the trenches, slit trenches, with the troops. . . right at ground zero. They were trying to find out how we would survive [battlefield nuclear weapons]," says Manuel. "People volunteered to go to Camp Desert Rock [in the '50s] because to get ahead in the Army you had to have certain credentials, like Atomic Warfare Training."

Adriano's health deteriorated rapidly beginning in 1958. He lived with chronic tiredness, blackouts and bone and muscle pain. He lost his teeth. In 1962 he had operations to remove his voice box because of cancer and 80 percent of his stomach. He developed leukemia and died from a heart attack in 1969.

Manuel remembers a Veterans Administration doctor saying: "He's another Camp Desert soldier. They're dropping off like flies."

Marthann Conner and son, Charlie

Marthann's husband, Bill, was a highly decorated bomber pilot in World War II. He was assigned to the 4926th radiation sampling squadron from 1957 to 1962. He participated in many sampling missions, flying around and through the mushroom clouds in Nevada and the Pacific. In the 1970s he began to have thyroid problems, numbness in his hands and legs and trouble with one leg. He was chronically tired and in pain the last years of his life. His thyroid was removed in 1982. Bill died on 5 April 1984. Cancer had spread throughout his body and he had spent his last ten months in the hospital.

"He was a very active, happy, optimistic, quiet man. Toward the end, he said, 'I just can't help but think the radiation is the cause of this.' We really had a good married life. We really enjoyed each other. We were devastated. We had planned on retiring and were looking forward to the next twenty years. Financially it is a real struggle."

Marthann's first pregnancy ended in a miscarriage. Her two sons have skin diseases and chronic environmental allergies. The younger son has dyslexia and had narcolepsy as a child.

Marthann works to support herself and her son, Charlie. She still seeks benefits from the Veterans Administration. She fears she will soon lose her home.

Colonel Langdon Harrison

Colonel Harrison was a pilot with the Air Force's 4926th Squadron for four years. The squadron was assigned to radiation sampling from 1949 to 1962. The pilots and aircraft of the 4926th, under the direction of Los Alamos Laboratories, collected air samples for analysis following atmospheric weapons tests. At times they were ordered to fly directly through the radioactive mushroom clouds. In Nevada, attempts were made to limit the pilot's exposure to radiation. Upon return to base after sampling missions, pilots were lifted from their aircraft by crane, stripped of their clothing and showered repeatedly. The aircraft were scrubbed down with high pressure hoses.

In 1956, Langdon was assigned with the 4926th to Operation Redwing, a series of seventeen nuclear detonations in the Pacific. His squadron was assigned to make repeated and protracted penetrations of the clouds from large hydrogen weapons immediately following detonation. Pilots were told at the time that they were intentionally being exposed to high levels of radiation. He remembers being told by Los Alamos officials of the risks of birth defects to children conceived after the operation.

This test of pilots and aircraft is officially labeled Human Experiment Number 133. According to film badges, air crews received at least 50 rem of radiation and cockpit instruments indicated exposure levels in the 100 rem range, higher than any previous level. As many as 25 aircraft were in the air after the large explosions. There were no decontamination procedures.

Langdon had surgery for cancer and his bladder was removed in 1985. During the course of his treatment he requested his service radiation records. He was told his total dose had been 8.2 rem. Because Langdon and other members of the squadron were required to monitor radiation levels as part of their duties, he knows that data existed recording much higher levels. "I had over 100 rem. I had all that data at one time, no one wanted it so we burned it all [before leaving the Pacific]." Langdon believes duplicates of the real Redwing data are still on file.

Casey and Susan Wnorowski

Casey served in the Navy and Air Force from 1945 to 1968. In 1956 his ship, the USS *Catamount,* was assigned to a series of 17 nuclear tests at Bikini and Eniwetok in the Pacific.

"We carried one of the hydrogen bombs aboard the ship. It was covered up, with Marine guards. Before the tests, a selected group was given training in decontamination: films, lectures, demonstrations and Geiger counters. We were to wash down the ship with salt water. I couldn't see the sense washing stuff off with water that you were in. We didn't know anything; they said there was no danger. I was in the deck force, always on topside. The one I remember most, it was 3 a.m. and it was like bright daylight, an airdrop, hydrogen. I thought it was something unimaginable, a hell of a thing to be involved in."

Casey's health had always been perfect. At the tests, he became sensitive to light, and has been photophobic ever since. Gastrointestinal problems began in 1957, back problems and leg cramps in 1958, headaches, blurred vision and blackouts in 1970. A benign brain tumor was removed in 1972; he regained motor control but remains numb on his left side. He has night sweats, lives with chronic fatigue and pain, suffers hearing loss and violent allergies. He had four healthy children before the tests. A son born in 1966 almost died at birth and has always been ill. He has seizures, problem with digestion and retarded growth, but he is intelligent and has a good attitude toward life. Casey has been unable to work since 1983.

"He's not a quitter. He believes in living life to the utmost," says Susan. "But he tires easily. He's not a complainer, but he expresses a lot of pain."

"I loved the military, and I'm very patriotic," says Casey. "I'm pissed. I think I've been used. I think they are lying to us. I think they should have told us. I wouldn't have done it then if I had known. From all I've read about it, they knew what was going to happen."

Pat Brody

Pat Brody's husband, Major Chuck Brody, was a crack Marine Corps pilot in World War II and Korea. In 1948 he was assigned to the Radiation Decontamination School on the aircraft carrier *Independence* in San Francisco harbor. The *Independence* was one of the target ships at Bikini in 1946 and highly contaminated with plutonium. He was on board for three days, eating, sleeping and working. His official radiation dose was zero.

In 1957 he was sent to Nevada, participating in shot Hood. Hood is the largest atmospheric test conducted within the United States, a 77-kiloton blast. Chuck was assigned to the front-line trenches, marched within 400 yards of ground zero, and spent several hours inspecting target houses, jeeps, tanks and animals.

Chuck's official radiation dose for Hood was 13 millirems, less than one-tenth of a 1950s chest X-ray. "Strange things happened," says Pat. "He had fainting spells, black outs, his teeth would break off. His abdomen enlarged and he would double over from pain."

In 1976 he was diagnosed with multiple, terminal cancers. He died in October 1977. Pat and Chuck saw a television program in 1976 about Paul Cooper, an atomic veteran dying of leukemia. It was their first realization that Chuck's problems might be caused by radiation exposure.

In the ten years since Chuck's death, Pat has filed nine claims for compensation with the Veterans Administration. All have been rejected. She has pursued her case in federal court, basing her argument on 'post-discharge failure to warn.' She asserted that the government acted in good faith during the testing, but at some point must have realized the veterans like her husband were becoming ill from their exposure and had a moral duty to warn them of the health consequences so they could seek appropriate medical care to prolong their lives. After ten years of hearings and appeals the government introduced a new defense, producing documents indicating that as early as 1945 the health dangers of nuclear testing were known and men like Chuck Brody were knowingly and secretly sacrificed. In February 1987, the court held for the government and dismissed Pat Brody's case.

"My government lied to me and boy, does that hurt. I am no longer your patriotic American citizen. I know too much. I still love my country; I no longer love my government. That is the memory I have of my government . . . humans used as an experiment."

Reason and Lois Warehime

Reason joined the Marines at age 16 in 1943. He fought in the battles of Saipan and Tinian, and his regiment, 5,000 men, landed in Nagasaki shortly after the atomic bomb was dropped.

"We stayed at the railway station. It was hard to believe one bomb had done all this. The Seabees and the 18th Engineers were running bulldozers most of the time. It was dry, dusty—lots of dust—we were sleeping in bags on the ground in pup tents. Nobody mentioned radiation. We stayed two weeks."

He was wounded four times in combat in the Pacific and Korea and was decorated for valor. He loved the military and became a top drill instructor. In 1953 he was assigned to Nevada and participated in Shot Simon as a platoon leader. Simon was a new, experimental weapon. It was expected to yield 23 kilotons, but in fact released over 50 kilotons. He estimates his platoon was 2,500 yards from Simon; eight officers were 500 yards closer.

"All I knew, it was going to be a big bang. You could see your bones, your whole body was compressed. The fireball was straight up and really big. The dust was so thick you couldn't see the guy next to you. When it cleared to 50 yards we moved in skirmish lines to our objective, through dead and blinded jackrabbits and coyotes. On the way back, a jeep with two safety monitors ordered us to get out. When we got back to our trucks we were dusted off with brooms. One hour after the shot everyone was sick and throwing up—54 guys. They took us to showers, ran Geiger counters over us, destroyed all our gear. We had diarrhea something awful. Two days later they sent me back to Fort Knox. My teeth came loose, I had to have them out. My hair fell out, then grew back. This shot ruined my military career. I have been tired ever since."

According to a Defense Nuclear Agency official, the eight forward officers are all dead.

Reason has skin cancer and rashes, cataracts, joint problems and muscle spasms and experiences night sweats. He has had blackouts and recurring fevers and was diagnosed as having lung cancer. He wears an electronic device to control the pain in his back.

Two sons were born to Reason and Lois after he was in Nagasaki. Both had bone, eye and joint problems, one also had a malformed liver. His grandchildren are sick all the time. "They have problems wrong with them they shouldn't have if they were four years old." He has been sterile since Nevada.

He has fought long and hard with the Veterans Administration to receive disability benefits based on his radiation exposure, so far without success. According to the Defense Nuclear Agency, he received only three rems total radiation, too little to warrant compensation.

"They should have compensated me long ago. I would have gone away and stayed quiet. I'll never stop fighting them now."

"He just had a frightening experience and realized how short life really was," says Lois. "We are having a financial struggle. With every VA appeal, you think maybe this time it will go through. It's very discouraging. He has been betrayed, by the promises made by the military that they take care of their own."

Jim and Jean Dennis

Jim Dennis was one of the Army's best. He was promoted from private in 1939, fresh out of high school, to lieutenant colonel, commanding a crack combat regiment. He fought with Patton in North Africa and Sicily, frequently behind enemy lines and became one of Patton's favorite young officers. Jim fought through the Philippines with MacArthur, entered Japan on one of the first planes, seeing the devastation at Hiroshima and Nagasaki. And he fought through the battlefields in Korea. He loved the Army and he loved commanding combat troops. He believes in the dictum, "Look after your men and they'll look after you." He became one of the Army's top explosives experts and many of the manuals he wrote in the 1960s are still in use today.

In March 1955, he was ordered to Nevada. He witnessed Shot Bee in the hours before dawn. He was in command of 300 men, at 3,500 yards from ground zero. They received no orientation; they had no respirators or film badges.

"The bomb was detonated on a 50-foot tower. With my hands covering my eyes, I saw the brightest light of my life. The earth felt like heavy seas, 60- to 70-foot waves. I could feel two shock fronts, with heavy fallout from the second. We were told [through loudspeakers] to stand up, turn around, look at the cloud. This was when we got hit in the face with fallout. It was sooty and made our hands, uniforms and faces black. I didn't pay attention to the soot because molten metal was dripping down through the stem, the most beautiful lavender stem. The tower was only half-vaporized and drooped over. I knew it was an incomplete detonation from my work with high explosives. A partial detonation is much dirtier than a clean burn.

"According to the official Defense Nuclear Agency record, we marched to 700 yards from ground zero and inspected equipment. But I walked directly to ground zero and everyone else did too. The troops were not afraid. Like me, they felt we were being cared for properly. We trusted them.

"I think the AEC, the Department of Defense and the government wanted to know how close they could get troops to weapons without killing us.

"The next day we witnessed Shot Ess, an underground explosion. The dust cloud was 10,000 yards across. It blanketed South and Southwest Utah. We returned by plane to our base. I had fever, headache, nausea, diarrhea, vomiting for two days. It recurred several months later. I've had dizziness, stomach pain, leg cramps, cardiac problems since 1955."

Jim left the military in 1960 and continued to work as an advisor and was later sent to work on a critical accident at the SL-1 military reactor at Idaho Falls, run by General Electric, "because of my detailed knowledge of explosives," says Jim. "The reactor had melted down, an uncontrolled fission chain reaction." His job was to place cutting explosive on the reactor, to break it into pieces small enough for burial.

"I was not told how dangerous the job was. I was given coveralls and a partial face mask. I worked for over nine hours one day on the reactor. Debris penetrated my face mask. They had me shower three times and ran a Geiger counter over me. I returned home."

Jim's health continued to deteriorate until finally he suffered a health crisis in 1977. "In November 1977, I woke up covered in blood. I am blind in one eye from the hemorrhaging. I almost died then and have had many crises since. " Jim has bone marrow and blood cancers. He has received chemotherapy and other treatments.

"I did not link my problems to radiation until 1978, when I began to hear about other veterans with similar problems. I first applied for VA benefits for radiation-induced cancer in 1978. I have been turned down many times. I filed a lawsuit against G.E. in January 1981 for my SL-1 exposure. It was my only remaining avenue. If I could have sued the government, I would have, because they loaned me to G.E. for the SL-1 cleanup.

"When I went to trial, the U.S. Department of Justice represented G.E. without showing any authority for doing so. They had up to 11 lawyers in court at one time. They brought in dolly-loads of documents. They had 32 expert witnesses, including one from Sweden, paying each of them a large daily fee. Some of their witnesses sat there for five weeks before they testified. They were being paid all that time. The trial lasted eight weeks. My presentation lasted seven days. Even though I was sick and terminally ill, the chief Justice Department attorney cross-examined me for two and one-quarter days. I felt he berated and insulted me, my witnesses and my wife. I lost the trial. I and others heard the Justice Department lawyers say they had a blank check to win this suit against us.

"At the end of the trial I felt like my life had ended. I felt there was no such thing as justice in this country. I wondered why I ever fought one day for my country. I think the government will take any action, spend any amount of money, to prevent anyone from winning a radiation injury or cancer suit."

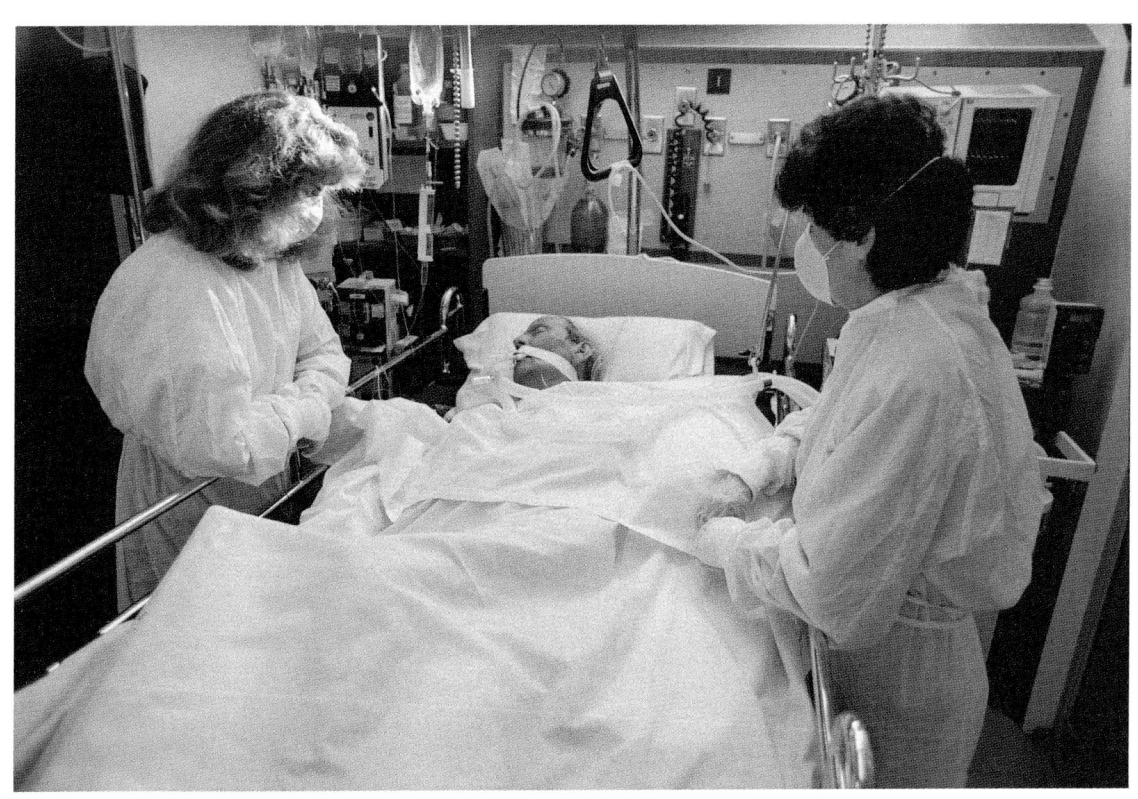

Announced U.S. Atmospheric Nuclear Tests

Year	Shot/Series	Location	Approximate number of participants	Film badging
1946	Crossroads	PPG*	42,000	Partial
1948	Sandstone	PPG	10,000	Partial
1951	Greenhouse	PPG	7,500	Partial
	Ranger	NTS**	500	Partial
	Buster-Jangle	NTS	6,500	Partial
1952	Tumbler-Snapper	NTS	10.000	Partial
	Ivy	PPG	12,000	Partial
1953	Upshot-Knothole	NTS	21,000	Partial
1954	Castle	PPG	10,000	Partial
1955	Teapot	NTS	8,000	Partial
	Wigwam	PPG	10,000	Total
1956	Redwing	PPG	10,000	Total
1957	Plumbbob	NTS	18,000	Total
1958	Argus	South Atlantic	4,500	Total
	Hardtack I	PPG	20,000	Total
	Hardtack II	PPG	1,000	Total
1962	Dominic I	South Pacific	28,000	Total
	Dominic II	NTS	3,000	Total
			222,000	

*Pacific Proving Ground
**Nevada Test Site

Source: National Research Council, May 1985

Who is the Enemy?

Dr. Karl Z. Morgan

Men in the military are trained to defend our country from attack and destroy the enemy. In the case of exposure to ionizing radiation, many servicemen today are asking who is the enemy? Why were we exposed? Is the Veterans Administration set up to help us who are suffering and dying from radiation exposure we were forced to receive in the line of duty?

Ionizing radiation is so called because it has sufficient energy to remove electrons from atoms or ionize them. It is measured in units of the rad (energy delivered corresponding to 100 ergs per gram) or in units of the rem. The rem and the rad are the same for X-rays, gamma rays and beta radiation, but in the case of alpha rays or neutrons, one rad = 20 rem. The man-rem is the average dose received by a given population multiplied by the number in this population. X-rays, gamma rays and neutrons are very penetrating and can pass through a man; beta rays of high energy can penetrate over a centimeter into the body surface while alpha rays cannot penetrate the protective layer of human skin. However, when alpha-emitting radio nuclides such as plutonium or americium are deposited inside the body, the exposure can be very serious. The alpha energy is about 10 times the average beta or gamma radiation, because each rad equals 20 rem and the long residence time in the body. For example, the residence time of plutonium in the human skeleton is 200 years, i.e. it would take 200 years for the body to remove half of it.

At very high single doses (over 20,000 rem) ionizing radiation can kill a person in minutes. The mid-lethal single dose is considered to be about 300 rem, meaning that about half such exposed persons would die of the radiation syndrome in a month.

The radiation exposure of our servicemen was from alpha, beta, gamma and neutron radiation and perhaps in every case less than the mid-lethal dose. Probably most of the officers that commanded men in the military to engage in operations that resulted in gamma and neutron doses of 10, 50, 100 to 200 rem and accumulated internal alpha doses of 500, 1,000 to 10,000 rem were not aware of its consequences. There is no question, however, but that those in higher levels of command were fully aware that such exposures would be expressed in symptoms of erythemia (skin reddening) and nausea

In the Shadow of the Cloud

shortly after exposure and would represent a high risk of radiation-induced cancer and other body ailments later in life.

I know this to be a fact because during this period I often had discussion of these risks with the commanding officers and other high ranking military officers during the tests. I was never able, however, to fully convince them of two major hazards: 1. Inhalation of radioactive particles, especially alpha-emitting particles such as those containing plutonium and, 2. External exposure to beta radiation. I was very concerned about the latter hazard and said so to my colleagues on board. We were stationed on the USS *Haven* and I made such a fuss about the fact that no measurements were made of the beta dose following tests Able and Baker that one of the high ranking military officers jokingly threatened to have me thrown overboard to the sharks. I was persistent and became such a nuisance that I was assigned a landing craft and six servicemen to make beta-dose measurements. We traveled to several of the Bikini Islands and boarded a large number of ships—both target ships and resident ships. We found that on the average the beta dose was three times the gamma dose and were shocked to discover that on some substances (tar, rope, rust, barnacles, etc.) the beta/gamma ratio was very high; the highest value measured was 600. I reminded the colonel that many of the men were sleeping nude top side on their ships in areas above five rem per hour because the temperature was above 100 degrees Fahrenheit, but I never knew if warnings were passed on to officers on the various ships and islands of the atoll. I also found very high gamma radiation levels in the boiler rooms and near sides of the ships and gave warning to the men whenever I had the chance.

Later I visited the San Francisco Navy Yard on two occasions and was not surprised at the high levels of radioactive contamination and the difficulties in decontaminating these ships. Those servicemen who resided on these ships and engaged in the renovation operations must have received very large doses, especially of beta external radiation and internal alpha radiation.

I attended numerous nuclear weapons tests at the Nevada Test site during the period of atmospheric testing. Here again I was rather frustrated. I knew one of the persons in charge of dosimetry, but he and others in charge gave very little consideration to internal dose (especially from alpha radiation) and external beta dose. Not only was measurement of these doses almost entirely lacking but few precautions were taken to minimize these doses. I was appalled when I learned that servicemen had been stationed in trenches only a few miles from ground zero and were ordered to hurry into the area of ground zero immediately after the weapons detonations. At the time of the flash, some of the

Who is the Enemy?

men could see the bones in their bodies and I calculated this corresponded to over 50 rem dose.

During some of the Nevada tests I had experiments under way at the test site to measure the dose at various distances from ground zero and in Japanese-type houses in order to determine the dose received by the Japanese survivors of the explosions at Hiroshima and Nagasaki. After an explosion my men would rush into the area in their trucks and retrieve our dose meters which were contained in steel balls. On one occasion I took part personally in the retrieval experiment. We drove our truck at top speed to the remains of the Japanese houses, located and threw on the truck the steel balls containing our instruments. We actually ran across the desert floor in this operation because of the high dose rate. We kept an eye on our rad-meter; it went off scale on the one rad per hour and we switched to the 10-rad-per-hour scale. In my case, it ran off this 10 rad per hour scale and, seeing a dark object ahead of me (probably a part of the weapons tower), I changed direction and the meter dropped back to less than 10 rad per hour.

Ionizing radiation is a very insidious and sneaky type of hazard. Single doses less than about 10 rad are not detected by the human senses but there have been many reports of human detection of flash doses in the range of 10 to 100 rad; above this the radiation syndrome begins—at higher doses in some and at lower in others. At flash doses of about 10 rad it is possible that many persons will sense a fluorescent light flash to the retina and detect a slight burning in the nose, probably due to the formation of ozone and nitrous oxide (the human sense of smell can detect only a few molecules).

I believe the radiation damage to the veterans was mostly of five types:

1. Beta dose erythema followed later by various forms of skin, muscle and glandular damage;
2. Cancer of many forms, especially lung carcinoma, colon cancer and brain tumors;
3. Lens cataracts due mostly to beta radiation;
4. Damage to the immune system (reticuloendothelial system) and a host of common diseases;
5. Genetic damage.

The beta doses (one and three above) may have been very high in some cases (up to 10,000 rad) and thus resulted in an early response (burning of the skin, like intense sunburn) and eye problems. Those who received very large doses had the usual symptoms of transepidermal injury (dry and wet dermatitis, blisters and painful raw wounds) after a week or two, but unfortunately the medical doctors had information only on the gamma dose and it was too low to be the cause of such symptoms.

In the Shadow of the Cloud

many of the short-lived fission products and induced radionuclides after a nuclear detonation have very high energy and correspondingly deep penetration into the body. For example, the maximum energy, half-life, soft-tissue penetration and source of some of the radionuclides that have a high yield are:

Radionuclide	Energy (MeV)	Half-Life	Range (mm)	Source
Br-84	4.68	31.8 min.	21	Fission
Rb-88	5.3	17.8 min.	23	Fission
Sr-91	2.67	6.67 hr.	13	Fission
Y-90	2.27	64 hr.	11	Fission
Y-92	3.63	3.53 hr.	16	Fission
Y-93	2.89	10.3 hr.	13	Fission
Y-94	5.0	20.3 min.	22	
I-132	2.12	2.26 hr.	11	
I-134	2.43	52 min.	13	
Te-133m	2.4	50 min.	12	
Na-24	4.17	14.96 hr.	18	from Na-23
P-32	1.7	14.28 days	8.5	from P-31
Cl-38	4.91	37.29 mos.	22	from Cl-37
Fe-59	1.57	45.6 days	8	from Fe-58
Co-60	1.55	5.26 yrs.	7.8	from Co-59

It is clear that these beta particles not only penetrate below the skin but reach the muscle, thyroid, many of the glands, and lymph nodes, the entire lens of the eye, and the male gonads. In the case of the male, the skin (epidermis plus dermis) thickness ranges from 1.1 to 1.9 mm on the thigh, 0.90 to 1.9 mm on the leg, 1.0 to 1.3 mm on the arm, 2.2 to 3.2 mm on the sole of the feet and 0.63 to 0.65 mm for the eyelid so the claim of some that beta radiation only radiates the skin is fallacious. The diameter of the eyeball through the center is 22 to 24.5 mm, so very little beta radiation reaches the retina.

Who is the Enemy?

However, the traverse diameter of the lens ranges from 9 to 10 mm so beta radiation of energy greater that 2 MeV penetrates the lens completely.

The standards setting bodies (International Commission on Radiological Protection, National Commission on Radiological Protection, United Nations Scientific Committee on the Effects of Atomic Radiation), the regulatory bodies (Nuclear Regulatory Commission, Department of Energy and Environmental Protection Agency) and the special National Academy of Science Committees (BEAR, BEIR-III) have consistently underestimated the risk of cancer from exposure to low levels of ionizing radiation. At present their risk estimates range from five cancers per 100,000 person-rem to five cancers per 10,000 person-rem. The more recent estimates are based on cancer incidence among the survivors of the atomic bombing of Hiroshima and Nagasaki. These studies underestimate the cancer risk for the reasons that follow:

1. Dose estimates were too high;
2. Neutron component of dose was grossly overestimated;
3. Use of low dose group as controls;
4. Cancer deaths still above normal;
5. An atypical population that was exposed to fire, blast, deprivation, psychological damage and severe damage to immune system—consequence:

    a. Those more prone to cancer die early of common diseases;

    b. Population of healthy survivors plus a population of persons with a damaged immune system.

The data on radiation workers at Hanford indicate a cancer risk of about five fatal cancers per 1,000 person-rem. I do not believe any value less than one fatal cancer per 1,000 person-rem can be justified at the present time (1987). Reports of the Government Accounting Office and more recently of Radiation Effects Research Foundation support a number of publications by Drs. A.M. Stewart, R. Bertell and myself showing that at low doses one can expect more cancers per rem than at high doses, so I expect that the value of five cancers per 1,000 person-rem is more appropriate for application to the gamma ray and neutron exposures of the veterans who were exposed. The reason one would expect a high incidence of radiation-induced lung and colon cancers among these exposed men is because of inhalation of dust-bearing radioactive material. A high prevalence of common diseases is expected

Who is the Enemy?

because of the serious damage to the immune system. Genetic damage from gonad exposure expresses itself not only on the children but on those to be born hundreds and thousands of years to come.

Finally, the Veterans Administration discounts radiation damage to the veterans because of the low recorded dose as provided by the film badges worn by some of the servicemen. These badges do not record the external beta and neutron dose, give no information on the internal alpha, beta and gamma dose and are only a poor estimate of the external gamma dose of the person wearing the badge. In many cases the badges were lost and the film ruined because of the high temperature and humidity and in some cases a badge was placed on only one in 20 of the men in the trenches who were hurried to ground zero. I have the horrible thought, what if some of these men not wearing a badge sat down on one of those "hot" objects I spotted on the desert floor that were reading over 10 rad per hour at five feet? The dose at contact could have been greater than 1,000 rad per hour and there would be no record of this dose! The Veterans Administration insists the servicemen's dose was no greater than two rem. Who is the servicemen's enemy?

Dr. Karl Morgan has been working with ionizing radiation for 56 years. He was one of the five first health physicists who were assembled at the University of Chicago during and shortly after the first man-made critical assembly of uranium and graphite in the west athletic stands at the University of Chicago, 2 December 1942. He was director of the Heath Physics Division of Oak Ridge National Laboratory for 29 years. He was a principal organizer of the Health Physics Society and the International Radiation Protection Association (more than 20,000 professional members in 1987) and the first president of both organizations. He has been a professor of health physics at four universities. He often is referred to as the Father of Health Physics. Dr. Morgan is a gentleman of the old school and a man of quiet warmth.

Patriots All

Dr. Susan D. Lambert

Albert Maxwell was a mountain of a man. He stood before me as he was leaving my office five years ago, tall and gentle, with the calm, knowing and forgiving eyes of a saint. As I watched him walk down the hall, it was hard to believe that this solid, assured man was riddled with multiple myeloma. Over the next five years, I and so many others who loved Al saw him become thin, stooped, ravaged. Unending pain etched his face. Al entered the Veterans Administration hospital for the last time in June 1986. Finally, after difficult, protracted weeks in intensive care, stupefied with pain and drugs but still fighting for life, Al died in February 1987. Jackie, his wife, was at his side, herself wasted away by the long death vigil.

Albert Maxwell was an atomic veteran. His death took him out of the ranks of American men who suffer from the physical and psychological trauma of nuclear weapons explosions. Over the past eight years, through personal interviews, letters and informal conversations, I have come to realize the depth of their suffering. The United States government knowingly exposed these men to ionizing radiation. As time has passed, and a myriad of health problems have become evident, the government is unwilling to support the veterans. Many reports have been published indicating that the radiation exposure levels were higher than previously stated. As yet, there has been neither an admission of responsibility, nor an offer of compensation. The atomic veterans feel betrayed by the country they have served. They are now stunned, hurt and angry.

The deepest problem that the atomic veteran faces is an unspoken one. It is a vein of uncertainty that runs through his life and manifests both personally and scientifically. On the personal level, the veteran who is ill faces the painful uncertainty of not knowing the exact nature of his illness. He constantly asks himself: "Was my illness caused by radiation exposure during participation in nuclear testing? How can I prove that my illness was caused by radiation, if indeed it was? What additional health problems may yet arise or be aggravated by my radiation exposure? Will I unwittingly pass on genetic defects to my children or grandchildren?"

There are also many atomic vets who are not ill, but who often express fear of developing cancer

Patriots All

or having genetically affected children. The latter fear runs so deep that some vets and their wives have consciously chosen not to have children.

These natural fears are endemic among atomic veterans. They yield implacable anxiety and mental unrest. And yet, as if this were not enough, there are more uncertainties—those imposed upon the atomic vet by science itself. It is no surprise that the veteran turns to the scientist for answers to the multitude of questions which plague him insistently.

Science has provided the tools and materials for the creation of the atomic bomb. Yet, when the veteran seeks answers from the scientific community, he encounters a formidable array of uncertainties. Scientists themselves cannot agree on many fundamental issues that directly effect the evaluation and outcome of a veteran's case.

Profound scientific controversies have been fueled by an unresolved debate among atomic scientists and medical researchers concerned with the medical effects of ionizing radiation. The following unanswered questions pose the major stumbling blocks confronting the atomic veteran:

- What is the dose that a given atomic veteran was actually exposed to?
- What is the best method to estimate the dose?
- What is the cancer risk at low levels of ionizing radiation?
- Is it possible to demonstrate a radiation causation in a given veteran using highly sophisticated lab tests?
- How does one take into account human variation when assessing the risk of radiation-induced disease in a given veteran?

The pressure of so much uncertainty leaves the atomic veteran bewildered. Out of his bewilderment the veteran gropes at both fact and fiction in the hope of unraveling and sorting out the complexities of his predicament. As a result, he often finds himself butting heads with his personal physician and waging verbal wars with the Veterans Administration and the Defense Nuclear Agency. His dilemma is like that of David facing Goliath, with one exception—his sling has no stone.

What valuable ammunition does the atomic veteran lack with which he might plead his case? Perhaps a profile of the common serviceman who became the atomic veteran would throw some light on this problem.

The soldiers were very young when they observed the nuclear tests. Most were in their late teens and early twenties. Although most men were drafted, many did look to the service for career

Patriots All

opportunities. The majority of them had not pursued education, or had been unable to find alternative employment. Others wanted to do something useful with their young lives until they matured enough to know the direction their civilian lives might take. Still others, overwhelmed by the natural confusion and fear of entering adulthood, enlisted in order to have a place to be—a place where they would learn a skill; a place where, if they obeyed orders and did what was expected of them, their lives would be relatively free of the unknown.

What was fundamentally similar in the character of these young men was that each entered the service innocent and patriotic. They were innocent of the nuclear specter—innocent of the delusion of omnipotence that was festering within the Department of Defense and the Atomic Energy Commission. They believed in the United States of America. They believed in its righteousness and benevolence and trusted that it would protect and guide them. They could not have known that their government, to whom they so willingly gave over their lives, would ever turn on them—especially in their time of greatest need.

The Nuclear Weapons Testing Program existed to improve the nuclear weapons capability of the United States. The Department of Defense knew that in order to have a sound nuclear capability it could not ignore the human element of its soldiers. The staggering power of a nuclear weapon would surely impact soldiers differently than would a conventional weapon. So the DOD not only had to train its soldiers in entirely new tasks, such as radiological safety, monitoring and clean up, but it saw that it would have to condition its soldiers psychologically to nuclear weaponry and its strategic and tactical use in a nuclear war.

The DOD message to the soldiers was clear: There is nothing to fear. Consider yourselves privileged in being given the opportunity to experience firsthand our country's unfathomable power. In military training films used in the 1950s, soldiers were told:

- "You can live through an atomic attack and live to fight another day."
- "This explosion is one of the most beautiful sights ever seen by man."

The men were reassured about the blast effect—that the shock wave traveled slowly enough to allow the men time to seek safety in their foxholes. They were also reassured about the heat—that burns would only occur if they were within a three-mile radius of ground zero, and then only to the exposed parts of the body. And they were told that radiation was "the least important effect"—that fatal radiation went up to only one mile.

Patriots All

For some of the soldiers these reassurances were effective. One atomic veteran, then a career serviceman, said that at the time he had a sense of making history. Numerous atomic veterans have said that an atomic bomb is indeed the most beautiful sight they have ever seen. An indelible impression was left on their minds of the unthinkable magnificence of the bomb's upward-rushing cloud, the very center of which was the world being turned inside out, and splayed across the sky. The compelling nature of power and supremacy plays easily on young minds. It is no small wonder that soldiers felt a strange, if disquieting, reverence for the bomb.

But there were other reactions. Some men stopped believing in God. One soldier, after seeing a blast at night light up the sky like a thousand suns, said that "only God could turn night into day." He had just witnessed a test, code-named Teak, at Johnston Island. It was a high-altitude burst in the megaton range that was reportedly seen 2,000 miles away. Men also tell how they could see the bones in their arms at the moment of detonation with their faces buried in the crook of their arm to protect their eyes from the intense light. One soldier peeped out of a tank hatch aboard a landing ship in the South Pacific and saw the complete skeletons of his fellow servicemen who were topside huddled together with sheets covering them.

For many soldiers the experience was devastating. They were afraid, but were even more afraid to express these feelings for fear of appearing unmanly. Atomic veterans have said such things as:

- "I lost all my love for life."
- "Life was no longer beautiful."
- "I felt lost."
- "People didn't look normal to me anymore."

One veteran has said that he was a 17-year-old boy who may have grown up too quickly.

Nuclear images haunt many atomic veterans. One veteran recounted to me a recurrent dream that troubles him to this day. In the dream he was driving alone late at night through Palmdale Desert, California. He saw bright lights and a group of people ahead of him on the road. Suddenly, without explanation, his truck began to roll and threw him violently to the ground. The impact broke his leg. The people he had seen on the road ahead of him were now all gathered around him. They looked dead "with the blood drained out of them." He was so terrified that he got back into his truck, dragging his broken leg and started to drive off. The veteran has told me that he feels that the "walking dead" in his dream are atomic veterans who have already died and are beckoning him to join them.

Patriots All

It is not a dream, but an unalterable fact that nuclear weapons testing took place in remote areas of the world—in vast oceanic spaces and uninhabited deserts—remaining out of sight of the mainstream of American awareness. A total of 235 atmospheric tests were conducted by the United States in the South Pacific and at the Nevada Test Site. At least 235,000 soldiers participated in those tests.

There is a striking common denominator among many of the atomic veterans. They feel as if they are tired, old men—men who have aged before their time. They speak of a lack of vigor, chronic fatigue and generalized, often debilitating, muscle pain. They often comment that they cannot keep up with their wives or with other people their own age.

But the atomic veterans are not old men. They are men in their late forties, fifties and early sixties with families of teen- and college-age children. They are men who were raised in a culture in which the man is the sole breadwinner and the primary decision maker of the family. Yet, it is these men who are now faced with the pain and frustration of not being the vigorous men they thought they would be. They often have physical symptoms that cannot be explained—certainly not for men of their age. Compounding the veteran's uncertainty about his health, he is often labelled a hypochondriac or told he has a psychosomatic disease.

The atomic veteran's story is told in the eyes of these men. The photographs in this book portray the fear, outrage, resignation and even hope that consume their daily lives. The atomic veterans are the quarter-million American men who, in the tender years of their lives, were ordered to witness and participate in the testing of nuclear weapons.

It was the 1950s. It was a time of innocence. It was a time when such an experience was a privilege to a young soldier. But today, both the innocence and the privilege have gone sour. The atomic veteran has been left alone—largely uncared for, uncompensated and underestimated. He is a ghost of our past. His plight, and ours, is a legacy of the atomic age. But by seeing him as he is portrayed in this book, by listening to him and heeding the message in his story, we will find that he can help us secure our future. His patriotism may not have been in vain, after all.

Dr. Susan Lambert has been performing physical workups and health research on atomic veterans and other groups exposed to radiation for the past eight years. She is Director of the Dodd Project for Radiation Studies in Boston. She is known to the veterans for her honest professionalism and her compassion.

Afterword

The question that has haunted me over the years I have worked with these veterans is how could this have happened in the United States? There are no easy answers, but happen it did, and the experience of these veterans raises profound questions for the future of all of us.

Beginning with the World War II Manhattan Project to develop the atomic bomb, most of the major decisions in the Nuclear Age have been made in secrecy, the greatest secrecy, clothed in the cloak of national security. From the earliest days, multi-billion dollar budgets have been at stake, and the atom promised unlimited power—for good or ill.

When World War II ended, the perceived threat to our national security did not end. We entered almost immediately into the Cold War. In 1947, the National Security Act was passed, imbedding into United States law for the first time the concept that covert decisions, policies and actions could be taken with only limited congressional oversight and without the knowledge or approval of the public, so long as those activities were deemed to be in the "national interest." It was a shortcut taken to ensure the survival of the United States in a dangerous world. It legally sanctioned the government and its agencies, among them the Central Intelligence Agency, the Atomic Energy Commission, and the Defense Nuclear Agency, to act in secrecy.

The great decisions of the nuclear age have almost all been made behind closed doors, with public support sought after the fact. The decisions to build the hydrogen bomb, to deliberately expose American troops to nuclear weapons testing, to expose the peoples of the Marshall Islands and Nevada and Utah to fallout, to continue large-scale underground nuclear testing after above-ground testing was banned in 1962, to subsidize the civilian nuclear power industry, with its promise of electricity "too cheap to meter," were made for us.

The soldiers and sailors in Nevada and the Pacific were told they would not be harmed by their exposure to radiation, although today's evidence indicates that some decisionmakers knew otherwise all along. We too, as civilians, are still told we are not being harmed by fallout and the universal contamination of the biosphere, by routine and accidental releases from power plants, by strontium, cesium and other radionuclides in the food chain. We are told the levels of exposure we receive are "safe."

Yet, the ailments of the atomic veterans often take many years to develop and are not easily recognized. Damage to the immune system subjects the individual to a host of illnesses long before cancer is manifest, and the immune system is the first casualty when strontium, cesium and plutonium

In the Shadow of the Cloud

enter our bones and continually irradiate the bone marrow. The genetic damage to the veterans' children is often subtle, but profound. We are less than 50 years into the nuclear age. Widespread atmospheric weapons testing began only 35 years ago; the era of large-scale nuclear power plants is only 20 years old. It is still too soon for the results to be fully manifest in mortality and longevity tables and in our lives. For this reason alone, the atomic veteran is so very important. His experience serves us as a model and a warning of a possible worldwide future, even without nuclear war. Why this happened is perhaps no longer the relevant question. That it did happen can no longer be reasonably disputed.

Today there are unresolved issues facing us in the Nuclear Age—space-based nuclear weapons, food irradiation, toxic radioactive waste being released into our environment, the effect of radiation on the human immune system—all needing our time and attention. Of all the issues facing us today, however, perhaps the greatest is our need to confront our individual and collective responsibility.

It has been a long journey together with these veterans for the past five years. When I began this project, many of the veterans felt isolated and forgotten. They thought their symptoms were unique and they had fallen through the cracks of the system, and their spirits were almost crushed. Today many of them and the surviving widows have linked together, recognizing the commonality of their plight. Many of them, like Reason Warehime, are now back out of their wheelchairs and sickbeds, although still terminally ill.

Many of the veterans I met have ceased feeling they are powerless victims without control over their lives. They now see the struggle they wage as being more than for themselves. They fight again for all of us, as veterans like Jim Dennis and Reason Warehime did in World War II and Korea. They have become survivors. They have gained a clearer vision of life.

The atomic veteran asks us to recognize his plight, to return to him his dignity, to provide him the medical care he needs, to keep his family from destitution, to provide for his widow and his children. In return, he offers us the chance to see where we are heading while there is still time. If we choose to see with clear vision, then perhaps the Nuclear Age can become an age of new awakening.

Publisher's Note

"We must care for those who have borne the battle, and for their widows and orphans."
—Abraham Lincoln

The United States has had a proud history of caring for those who sacrificed their bodies, their health and their lives fighting for our country, its principles and ideals. This obligation to care should extend to all those who have served, whether in active battle in any corner of the world or on the testing grounds of military research.

Unfortunately for the atomic veteran, acknowledgment of and recompense for their physical sacrifice has been slow in coming. The United States government denies any correlation between the exposure to radiation atomic veterans received while in military duty and the majority of illnesses—leukemia and other cancers—they suffer today. Instead, those who bore the brunt of atomic weapons testing in Nevada and the South Pacific are faced with laws and policies that effectively prevent them and their survivors from obtaining the disability or death benefits other veterans receive.

First, the Feres Doctrine prohibits servicemen from filing suit against the government for injuries or abuses sustained while in the armed forces (see *Feres* v. *United States*, 340 US 135, 1950). Atomic veterans' suits for illnesses they contend result from exposure to radiation effects from atomic weapons testing are dismissed. The Warner Amendment, passed through Congress in 1984, accorded the same immunity retroactively to all private contractors that took part or were associated with the atomic weapons testing program.

Second, veterans and soldiers are limited to paying no more than $10 for legal help in preparation of disability claims to the Veterans Administration (see 38 USC ss3404-5). This fee limitation, established after the Civil War, was challenged as being unconstitutional by the National Association of Radiation Survivors (NARS), representing over 5,000 atomic veterans. Although the law was not found unconstitutional by the Supreme Court in 1985, the hearing did open the path to allowing a trial on the 1864 law in Federal District Court. The trial was held in San Francisco in 1987; a decision is expected in mid-1988. Any verdict is likely to be appealed.

Third, the Veterans Administration is the sole and final arbiter of the veterans' claims and the decisions cannot be appealed in federal court, according to another federal statute passed in 1934 (see

In the Shadow of the Cloud

38 USC s211a). Of the more than 8,000 radiation illness claims made to the Veterans Administration by atomic veterans, only 37 have been granted. Another 700 claims are pending while 7,300 have been denied as of October 1987, according to NARS. During the court hearing on the $10 fee limitation, the Veterans Administration was fined $135,000 by Judge Marilyn Hail Patel for shredding documents requested by the court. It has been contended that the documents would have shown that some Veterans Administration employees denied benefits lawfully due veterans (see *The New York Times,* December 7, 1986 and June 12,1987). A Justice Department lawyer told *The New York Times* that the taxpayers will have to absorb the penalties imposed on the agency. During the NARS trial, the Veterans Administration was also fined thousands of additional dollars for witholding internal documents sought by the veterans group, and was found to have made "false and misleading statements" that it was in compliance with court mandates (see *The New York Times,* June 12, 1987).

Some atomic veterans and veterans organizations such as NARS question the accuracy or veracity of information they receive when they request their official exposure dosages. The Veterans Administration and the Defense Nuclear Agency are the only available official sources for information on the exposure dosages received during military duty. The veteran must rely on these estimates or records of exposure when they make their claims. The estimated dosages the government reports are almost always less than the five rems considered safe by the Atomic Energy Commission, according to NARS. A United Press International article in 1982 reported that a former Army medic, breaking 25 years of silence, said that he "was ordered to enter false data to hide the fact that soldiers at four atomic tests in 1956 and 1957 were exposed to dangerously high levels of radiation."

"We were instructed to keep two sets of books," the medic reported to UPI. "One set was to show that no one received an exposure above the approved dosimeter reading. The other set of books was to show what the actual reading was." (See *The New York Times,* Feb. 8, 1982.) The Department of Energy, successor to the Atomic Energy Commission, denied the allegations.

The atomic veteran is left with few sources of assistance. His own government has turned away and denies his claims for care and for help. Despite President John F. Kennedy's wish, as he announced the end of U.S. atmospheric testing to the nation in July 1963, that, "The loss of even one human life or the malformation of even one baby. . . should be of concern to all of us. . . . ," the atomic veteran is still waiting for expression of that concern.

Publisher's Note

For more information on atomic veterans, the atomic weapons atmospheric testing program and legislation pending in Congress on atomic veterans issues, the following addresses and bibliography may be of help:

National Association of Radiation Survivors
942 Market Street, Suite 710
San Francisco, CA 94102
(415) 397-2001

National Association of Atomic Veterans
11004 E. Highway 40
Independence, MO 64055
(816) 737-9434

International Alliance of Atomic Veterans
P.O. Box 32
Topock, AZ 85436
(602) 768-7515

House Armed Services Committee
2120 RHOB
Washington, D.C.
(202) 225-4151

Senate Veterans' Affairs Committee
414 RSOB
Washington, D.C.
(202) 224-9126

Suggested Reading

Ball, Howard, *Justice Downwind*, Oxford University Press, New York, 1986

Brown, Anthony Cave and MacDonald, Charles B., *The Secret History of the Atomic Bomb*, The Dial Press, New York, 1977

Doyle, Christine M., "Government Liability for Nuclear Testing under FTCA," University of California, Davis, *Law Review* 15, 1982

Hugghe, Patrick and Konigsberg, David, "Grim Legacy of Nuclear Testing," *The New York Times Magazine*, April 22, 1979

McCarthy, Shirley, "VA Defends Politics, Not A-Bomb Victims," *Washington Post*, August 4, 1980

Rosenberg, Howard, *Atomic Soldiers*, Beacon Press, Boston, 1980

Saffer, Thomas H. and Kelly, E. Orville, *Countdown Zero*, G.P. Putnam's Sons, New York, 1982

Smyth, Henry DeWolf, *Atomic Energy for Military Purposes: The Official Report on the Development of the Atomic Bomb under the Auspices of the U.S. Government, 1940–1945*, Princeton University Press, Princeton, N.J., 1945

Wasserman, Harvey and Solomon, Norman, *Killing Our Own*, Delacorte Press, New York, 1982

"Atomic Test Effects in the Nevada Test Site Region," Atomic Energy Commission, January 1955

"Exercise Desert Rock VII and VIII: Final Report of Operations," by the staff of Headquarters, U.S. Sixth Army, November 1957

"Discussion of Radiological Hazards Associated with a Continental Test Site for Atomic Bombs," minutes of a meeting held at the Los Alamos Scientific Laboratory, Los Alamos, N.M., August 1, 1950

"Troop Participation in Operation Tumbler-Snapper," report of the Director, AEC Division of Military Application, March 1952